The mixed border

Cover: Mixed border in Pamela Milburne's Kent garden, late July. Phloxes predominate, including 'Norah Leigh' with variegated foliage in foreground. White *Escallonia* 'Iveyi' at back is framed by golden-variegated *Elaeagnus pungens* 'Maculata'. Spiky *Eryngium decaisneanum* (*E. pandanifolium*), left, will rise to 7 feet when flowering in autumn.

Overleaf: *Clematis* × *jackmanii* 'Superba' threaded through a buddleia.

The mixed border

A Wisley handbook

Christopher Lloyd

Cassell Ltd
The Royal Horticultural Society

Cassell Ltd.
1 Vincent Square
London, SW1P 2PN
for the Royal Horticultural Society

First published 1986

British Library Cataloguing in Publication Data

Lloyd, Christopher, 1921–
　The mixed border. — (A Wisley handbook)
　1. Perennials
　I. Title　　II. Royal Horticultural Society
　III. Series
　635.9′32　　　SB434

ISBN 0-304-31093-X

Photographs by Christopher Lloyd
Frontispiece by Michael Warren
Design by Lynda Smith
Phototypesetting by Georgia Origination Ltd, Formby
Printed by Het Volk n.v. Ghent, Belgium

Contents

Introduction

The mixed border is the natural successor, in the evolution of garden history and practice, to the herbaceous border, to the border for annuals and tender plants, and to the shrubbery. Additionally, it gives us new scope for the use of bulbs.

Mankind has ever shown a tendency to categorise and pigeon-hole. This is natural when you are feeling your way into a new subject, and the experience of an individual is also the experience of a nation.

Coming fresh to gardening, you feel the need to anchor yourself to something; some flower, most likely. It may be roses. 'We must have a bed of roses', you'll say. Or of heathers or of conifers or perhaps, rather daringly for a beginner, of the two combined.

But when you mature, intellectually speaking, you come to realise that monocultures, though simple to grasp as a concept, are unnecessarily restrictive. To grow none but herbaceous plants together in a border, for instance, means that it will lack the substance and firmness of texture that could be introduced by shrubs, as it will also lack the continuity of colour provided by tender bedding plants. Why not enjoy the best features and examples of these different categories by combining them in a judicious mixture?

Opposite, top to bottom: Lupins interplanted with *Tulipa* 'Halcro', late May. Same view, mid-June, with lupins in flower. Lupins succeeded by *Malope trifida*, *Verbena bonariensis* in foreground, 21 Oct.
Below: *Malope trifida*, showing green translucent calyx at flower base.

Another and very practical advantage in the mixed border is that it avoids the dramatic build-up of pests and diseases that you will always find in monocultures. It is no accident that roses attract a longer list of these afflictions than any flower we grow. It is because so many of us are growing roses in gardens or beds devoted to them alone, that their pests and the pathogens causing their diseases can so easily build up to epidemic proportions. In a mixed border this can never happen. The pest that will attack one plant will find its neighbour distasteful. Roses are excellent mixed border plants. You'll not be able to grow so many of them as in a rose border but you will be able to grow a much wider variety of plants, and variety is truly the spice of life. The older I get the less I want to specialise, because specialisation is the enemy of variety with all its riches.

There is nothing new about the mixed border. Many of us have long been caring for or achieving one while calling it herbaceous. But in the long run the herbaceous border has earned itself a bad name as representing a singularly costly and lavish style of gardening that is closed to all but the rich (which generally means some public authority or institution, these days, caring for a historic garden like Hampton Court). I think it is the word herbaceous, in all its clumsiness, that puts people off the concept. Even if you drop the h, American style, and say 'erbaceous, you're no better off. And do you talk about an 'erbaceous border or a herbaceous border or a cross between the two? Many authors write an 'herbaceous border' but I doubt if they ever speak it like that.

Gertrude Jekyll never, in my reading of her, referred to her borders as herbaceous. 'I have a rather "mixed border of hardy flowers" ', she wrote in the late 1890s. 'It is not quite so hopelessly mixed as one generally sees, and the flowers are not all hardy.' That seems a pretty good mix to me.

A point worth remembering is that categories like shrub, herb, annual, biennial and bulb are merely terms coined for our own convenience. The plants themselves know nothing about them and often fall between two categories, in which case we need to compromise, rather lamely, by calling them sub-shrubs or short-lived perennials. We blithely classify cyclamen and anemones (some of them) as bulbs, but would leave out the agapanthus because it cannot be dried off and stored like other bulbs, although its close relationship to accredited bulbs like nerines, crinums and amaryllis is clear for all to see.

In nature, plants mix all the time, so why not in the garden? In a mature piece of woodland you'll find a tree canopy, a layer of shade-tolerating shrubs beneath that, and beneath them, again, herbs like trilliums, dog's-tooth violets, Virginian cowslips and anemones; plants which can complete all their flowering and growing in the early months of the year when there is plenty of light reaching them and before the trees and shrubs have put on their leaves. There is much we can learn from this.

SIZE AND SHAPE

A border can be of any size or shape. The advantage of plots that are freely intersected by paths is that you can reach every plant without stepping on the border. For a cottage-style garden this works well enough but my own recommendation would be to make, where given the opportunity, one large border in preference to several small ones. It means that you can use larger growing plants without upsetting the balance. Tall plants look ridiculous in a small border. It also means that you have scope for grouping some of your plants, which looks so much more effective than dotting them singly all over the place. This is the cottage garden tendency; one that can look charming, but is often a fidgety mess that allows the eye nowhere to rest.

Another fidget to avoid – yet how frequently you see it – is a fussy outline to a border. Where you use curves make them long, smooth and easy, not short, crimped and wiggly. Curves should appear inevitable and not to have been made for their own sake in an 'I love curves' orgy. Straight lines within a formal or architectural setting will often look appropriate and are nothing to be ashamed of. Your plants themselves can break up the line of a hard edge by lapping over it.

YOUR BORDER'S SEASON

A shrub like a yucca can look pretty good (if you like it in the first place) at all times of the year, but most plants have a seasonal peak, outside which they are at best inoffensive but still mere passengers. Others, in their dormant period or when we are tired of them, disappear from the scene altogether.

When planning a bed – and it is always better planned than tumbled into – you should have a definite peak season in mind, during which none of the contents is looking sordid or disreputable.

Let us say (as I choose to make it) that this period is from mid-June to mid-August. That's two months, and to expect longer at high pressure is both greedy and unpractical. But you can, as I shall show, include earlier interest without diluting the main impact and you can also do much to prolong the display into autumn.

There are so many plants to choose from that it is a positive advantage to impose restrictions on ourselves in one way or another. One such is that a plant's season of beauty should not be

Early June, with pink *Weigela florida* 'Variegata', Dickson's golden elm behind.

too short. I will take *Lychnis chalcedonica*, sometimes called the Maltese cross, on account of the notch at the tip of each petal, as an example. This 3 to 4 foot hardy perennial carries domed heads of pure scarlet in July. It is a rare and, to those not frightened of handling it, an invaluable colour to find in a perennial at this season (it occurs in the oriental poppy a month earlier). The snag is that it lasts a mere two weeks, and whatever treatment you give the plant afterwards, it will have nothing more to offer. In a large border you can accommodate a few, but only a few, passengers like this. You could plant in front of it a later developer like *Verbena bonariensis* or *Cimicifuga racemosa*, which would raise itself above lychnis level after the latter had made its bow.

Such problems and working out the best solutions are the very stuff of creative gardening and only next in importance to growing a plant well in the first place.

There are some devices for prolonging a border's season which are perfectly simple; other that are labour intensive in the extreme. Most popular writing on our subject today concentrates on labour saving (low maintenance, the Americans call it), and that's fair

Late August, *Crocosmia* 'Citronella' in front of weigela, *Aster sedifolius* (*A. acris*) left, *Salix alba* 'Argentea' with elm.

enough when you are addressing reluctant garden owners. But we are a nation of gardeners such as exists nowhere else in the world and we have the best of all climates for our purpose. So it is nothing to apologise for if we enjoy labour when it is productive of something rather special.

Suppose you had a sitting out area and, behind that, a window to look from in less clement weather. Your view might well be of a mixed border designed in a broad, curving sweep with a hedge or evergreen shrubs behind it to form a background. I would still recommend that you aim at a limited season for that border's peak, but I would also suggest that you stick at nothing to prolong it by all manner of 'cheating' (as some would describe it but I'm not about to recommend plastic flowers or celluloid models of pink flamingoes), especially if you have a back-up area in the way of spare ground, a greenhouse or cold frames in which to keep plants in reserve until they are needed.

Patches of early flowering annuals in your border could then be replaced by others, moved in at the critical moment from the reserve. And not only annuals. Perennials like doronicums,

Achillea 'Moonshine' or *A.* × *taygetea*, pyrethrums, epimediums, astilbes or anything else with an easy-going, fibrous root system, can be moved to a spare row after flowering and be replaced for a late summer and autumn display by other perennials of a similar root system. Such are *Aster* × *frikartii*, *A. amellus* and all the traditional michaelmas daisies; similarly chrysanthemums of the Korean and other sufficiently early flowering types. Perennial lobelias (*L. fulgens*, *L. cardinalis*, *L. vedrariensis*, *L. syphilitica* and cultivars derived from them) are good movers even as late as August, when coming into flower. Hebes move beautifully and especially suitable are the most glamorously flowering but somewhat tender kinds like 'Andersonii Variegata', 'Simon Delaux', 'Evelyn' and 'La Séduisante'. Theirs is a 3 to 4-months-long season, particularly if you snap the dead spikes off as they run to seed. There are many other possibilities and you can experiment for yourself.

The one essential for success is to do the job properly. This, in most weathers, will entail a heavy watering the day before moving of everything that's to be moved, whether into or out of your border, followed by a further liberal watering after planting, to settle them in. If, at this stage, the water is liable to pan the surface and run off it, I prefer to puddle the plants in. That is to say, I dig my hole, set the plant in it, pour over its roots anything up to a gallon of water, quickly from an upturned watering can, and then, as that is draining but not quite drained away, scoop in the soil to fill the hole.

Such practices sound like and are a lot of work; interesting work but undeniably time and effort consuming. So to the question which will be put sooner rather than later 'are mixed borders labour saving?', the answer is that they can be, but that the greater the inputs the greater the outputs. The most sensible course to adopt is to use some plants that will do the work for you by covering the ground, suppressing weeds and looking mildly agreeable over a long season. The time thus saved can then the more willingly be devoted to other plants which will yield even greater rewards, but only if you take trouble over them. The balance can be tilted one way or the other according to how well you are feeling, how keen on the garden, how involved in other matters and what help you can muster.

THE SITE

A site open to sunshine (given our climate) but protected from wind, is to be preferred. However, there are many shade loving plants, so long as it is not the dense, dry, rooty shade brooded over by trees like beech or cherry. Few plants worth having will grow happily under them and it is certainly no place to start a mixed border.

Wind protection is not essential but makes life more comfortable for you as well as for the plants. On a windy site you must use lower growing plants. Those with grey felted leaves are particularly well adapted to wind, if it is not icy from the north or east.

A southerly aspect is ideal for a one-sided border. Its background, whether wall, fence, hedge or shrubs, will protect it from the coldest winds. A north-facing border can be managed but the chief disadvantage, since it will be viewed from the north, is that all the plants will be leaning and, in many cases, turning their leaves and flowers towards the south. In those that are anyway shade loving like nicotianas, busy lizzies, begonias, cimicifugas, border phloxes, ferns, fatsia and aucuba, this would not be noticed. It's a matter of making the right choices.

There is no question of aspect for an island bed that receives ample light from every direction. The main problem here is backgrounds dark enough to highlight the flowers. These backgrounds can, if sufficiently tall, as on rising ground, be at a considerable distance from the border they are highlighting.

Paved or other hard margins to your borders will be the most satisfying, as they'll allow the pool and cushion forming plants to spread forward in a pleasantly relaxed manner during their growing season, which also effectively adds to the width of a border. I personally feel no scruples about allowing my plants to lap on to a lawn in summer, as I loathe the cliff-like edge and sterilely empty strip of earth that prim-minded gardeners enforce between a lawn and the first plants in a border. Plants don't seem to be enjoying themselves under this regime and I cannot enjoy them. You can perfectly well manage the lawn grass next to an overlapping plant, if you want to, and the bare patch left by the plant at the end of the growing season will soon fill in, even if only with annual meadow grass. Lawns should be considered an adjunct to borders and not an end in themselves.

PREPARATIONS FOR A NEW BORDER

Never be in a hurry when making a new border. Adverse basic factors are far easier to remedy before it has been planted, so you may well need to allow a year, which will include an entire growing season, in which to make ready. But I am not about to recommend double digging. That is quite unnecessary.

Good drainage even in the wettest weather is all-important. Plants can't swim and they can all too easily drown. If in any doubt, lay tile drains and don't put them in too deep, otherwise the water

that is afflicting your plants may never reach the drains. They need be no deeper than 12 to 15 inches, which is below the depth you'll want to dig in the course of ordinary cultivations.

If the garden adjoins a recently completed house, the chances are that the builders will have dumped the subsoil from their excavations on top of the natural soil in your garden. Nothing will grow in subsoil. It must be removed. If the garden needs landscaping, then its top soil must be set on one side while the alterations are made, and returned at the end. It is often desirable to bring in additional top soil from another building site, with which to make good your own losses.

What kind of soil are you dealing with? If light, it will have the advantage that you can do what you like on it half an hour after heavy rains at any season of the year. It will drain easily and be easy to work. But it will dry out quickly and will probably be short of water-retentive organic matter. You'll need to add this, right through the border's life, in generous quantities. Rather coarse sedge peat has excellent physical properties. So has bark, but if this is fresh it should be stacked for a year before use, otherwise it takes nitrogen from the soil in the course of decomposition and will thus deprive your plants. It's the same story with any raw organic

14

Opposite: *Geranium psilostemon* supported by *Crambe cordifolia*, with spikes of foxglove and mullein.
Above: *Geranium endressii* 'Claridge Druce' mingles with *Cornus alba* 'Elegantissima'.
Below: *Geranium sanguineum* knits into pale yellow *Achillea* × *taygetea*.

matter. Farmyard manure, if it smells ammoniacal, is still not ready for use on ground that is shortly to be, or has already been, planted. But you can dig it into a border in autumn that will not be planted until the next year. Well decayed garden compost is good and there are a number of other possibilities according to availability in the area where you live.

Heavy soils are water retentive which is a good thing if you have their drainage under control. You can permanently improve their physical properties by the addition of large quantities of grit, which is crushed shingle and is of a coarser texture than any natural sand. Spread it so thickly that, before digging it in, the soil beneath is invisible. You may have difficulty in finding a supplier in your locality; builders' merchants are the best bet. Fertility, as always, will be improved by the addition of decayed organic matter, which is humus.

If weeds, especially docks and nettles, are growing luxuriantly on your plot when you come to it, this is a good sign and indicates high fertility, without which you will never be successful, but you must get rid of them all the same. Indeed, you must make sure of having wiped out all perennial weeds in a border before you start to plant it up, otherwise their recurrence from dormant roots will give you endless trouble. When these weeds are growing strongly, treat them with glyphosate, which is marketed as Roundup (wholesale) or Tumbleweed (retail). It is non-residual in the soil but systemic in the plants treated, destroying their roots as well as the visible portions sprayed. A second application may be necessary in the case of very persistent weeds like ground elder.

Immediately prior to planting (generally in autumn or spring but there is no dead season, except as imposed by the weather) get the top soil into a friable condition that will make it easy to settle around plant roots. You can either fork it over, breaking lumps down with the back of your fork as you go, or you can use a mechanical cultivator.

If you are planting to a scale plan, you'll need to transfer it to the border with the help of a string grid, thereafter marking in the outline plants with a cane and a label. Or you may prefer to work on an *ad hoc* basis, having collected a reservoir of plants in a spare plot during the months or year in which you were making the site ready.

With an original plan you'll make fewer mistakes in the first instance, because you'll have had time to work out colour juxtapositions and relative plant heights but you'll make plenty of mistakes however you set about it. The great thing is not to mind admitting them and to change things round when you see what's wrong. All gardening involves constant change and your border should never be complete but always in a state of evolution.

Do make groups as well as planting singletons, especially in the first instance, when you're starting with empty ground and you're not yet cramped for space in which to grow all the treasures you long to possess. Even with shrubs, a group of something like *Potentilla fruticosa*, *Caryopteris* or *Perovskia* will look the more effective for not just being dotted around. With plants, even more so. A single phlox is meaningless. You need to see a mass of it to create a plushy impression. The same with cushions of *Sedum* 'Autumn Joy' or *S. spectabile*.

RESTRICTIONS ON PLANT CHOICE

I have already pointed out the joy of there being so few restrictions imposed upon you as to what you may grow in a mixed border. Even cacti (some opuntias are hardy) can be included if they appeal to you.

But there are certain limitations imposed from without and others by personal choice and preference.

From without, climate, soil and availability are the most obvious. The foliage shrub, *Gleditsia triacanthos* 'Sunburst', which I grow in a mixed border in Sussex would not thrive for anyone north of the midlands. Its young wood does not ripen enough in the summer to carry it through the following winter. Similarly there are autumn flowering plants, like certain pampas grasses, that do not develop their flowers in time before the growing season comes to an end, while the wood of *Camellia japonica* cultivars is apt not to ripen sufficiently, given cool summers, to bud up well for next spring's flowering. These are typical climate limitations.

In respect of soil, the most obvious and best known is the fact that on alkaline (limy, chalky) soils, such plants as rhododendrons, camellias, many meconopses and heathers will not grow. Others, like hydrangeas, will develop bright yellow foliage and not grow too well, though it may be possible to keep them happy by applying regular doses of iron Sequestrene. On the whole it is sensible (and dignified) to grow the plants that your soil suits (there'll always be plenty of them) and not wring your hands over the rest.

Another big moan is always sent up when a plant that you have read about in the press is not available from your local garden centre. There's no such thing as an unobtainable plant, but you have to search around (for pity's sake enclose a stamped, addressed envelope when badgering someone with enquiries). If you join an organisation like the Hardy Plant Society, you'll be in on plant and seed exchanges of rare items. If you're a member of the Royal Horticultural Society, it will help if it can. But if a plant remains unobtainable for the time being, console yourself with the thought that your border can only accommodate a tiny fraction of the vast number that *are* available.

For this reason it may sometimes please you to impose your own restrictions, the commonest being to limit the flower and plant colours in your border. All-grey-and-white is very popular, with a bow towards Sissinghurst Castle as the fashionable prototype. Some people are crazy on blue flowers. Unfortunately they usually mix in those with mauve and purple in their make-up and this is a mismatch. Blue anyway looks rather dead on its own and is much livelier when combined with yellow or pink or white. All-yellow borders look good and can include plenty of variegated foliage. Many gardeners are nervous of misusing yellow, in case it clashes unacceptably with bright pink or magenta. All-yellow is a way out of this, but yellow and white is even better, I think.

For myself, I am happy with a complete mixture, though I do watch what's going immediately next to what. The bright pink of rose 'Zéphirine Drouhin' will look happier next to spikes of blue delphiniums than in the company of a yellow daisy like *Buphthalmum (Telekia) speciosum*.

A MIXED BORDER IN MATURITY

Before going on to consider the different types of plants used in mixed borders in greater detail, I will make some general remarks on upkeep.

It will never be necessary, unless you have allowed the weed problem to get out of control, to take everything out of the border and start again, as is the routine recommended for herbaceous borders every 6 years or so.

All work in a mixed border will be on a piecemeal basis. Where perennials are in question, organise matters so that they don't all reach the stage of needing to be divided and re-set simultaneously. Otherwise your border will look weak in the following summer.

But I like to go right through a border, examining and, if necessary, attending to its components once a year. The main time for this can be in autumn or in spring. I used to be an autumn over-hauler but now prefer spring – March, to wit. The days, then, are not so aggravatingly short as in autumn and perhaps you are, on average, less frequently interrupted by rain. Also you can see where the bulbs are and avoid them. Herbaceous rubbish that you carry away is paper light by then.

To leave certain plants that will eventually need cutting right down looking derelict until the spring may be a worry, especially if your border is constantly within your sight lines. Mine is not and I'm quite well trained, by now, not to notice what I don't want to see, but only in the dormant season when the garden is little frequented. And many skeletons that look derelict at one moment may suddenly be transformed by frost or snow into objects of beauty.

One of the advantages of the mixed border in winter is the variety of shapes and colours that it still retains at that season, even when there's no flower to be seen.

Whether you cut your plants down in autumn or in spring, I would advise you never to do it until you are ready to deal with that piece of ground – weeding, planting, splitting, dividing and replanting or whatever. It is far easier to remember how your plants grew; indeed, to remember what they are, while their skeletons are before you. You also need to recollect how they stood in relation to one another. You can act logically only if you know these things. Furthermore, the ground beneath plants that have not been cut down is largely protected from the slimy conditions imposed by rain and frost. Deal with a little stretch of border at a time; then another stretch. Finish each stretch before the night's rain or frost sets in.

The time for the pruning, thinning or trimming of shrubs will vary but it is often possible to get on with some of this, like the pollarding of willows or the cutting back of some other foliage shrub such as the golden cut-leaved elder, in the depths of winter when the ground is too hard for planting, weeding or cultivating. Where I live I like to prune my roses in winter too. With most of them it is principally a question of thinning out old branches.

While the ground is still wet, you should apply your surface, moisture-retaining mulches, whether of decayed leaves, peat, bark, garden compost or whatever. In March, we put on a surface dressing of chicken manure well decayed in sawdust. We have a deep litter chicken house, from which this comes. As this manure is always kept under cover until actually used, it is rich in nutrients but devoid of weed seeds, which is a great advantage. Even so we add a balanced dressing of general fertilizer at this season, containing nitrogen, phosphorus and potassium, at 4oz to the square yard. This gives the newly growing plants a boost. You may prefer a slower-acting organic fertilizer like hoof-and-horn. My chicken manure is the slow-acting side of it.

By May, some of your plants will need supporting. If the site is really open, you will require more support but the plants less. The irony of this situation is explained by the fact of an open, sunny situation inducing stocky, wind resistant growth. In sheltered and particularly in one-sided borders, the plants become drawn. Still, it's usually the best way to give them a background and this is therefore a situation to be tolerated.

Always leave enough space – say 15 inches – between groups of plants in a border, to allow you to move between them without leaving a trail of damage. This will not prevent the foliage from joining up between groups. The indecency of earth visible in high summer should never be tolerated, but that is no excuse for congested planting.

How you support your plants will partly depend on what you can find. We use hornbeam or hazel peasticks for such as monarda, *Salvia nemorosa* 'Superba', *Alstroemeria ligtu* hybrids and *Aster sedifolius* (*A. acris*). But you could make a job of it with canes and a cat's cradle of fillis, which is soft, fawn-coloured string, stretched between canes, starting and finished with a clove hitch. Five-ply fillis is the right strength to last a season in most cases.

I always use the canes and fillis technique with stemmier plants such as *Achillea filipendulina*, *Aconitum* 'Sparks' and the tall wild prototype of *Phlox paniculata*. With a clump of delphiniums you can usually get by with a triangle of canes (knock them in straight and with the broad end downwards), passing the fillis with a twist around each delphinium stem on the way to hitching it at each cane. Wait till you can do this at the 3 to 4 foot level and you'll only need the one tie, using strong, 5 foot canes. Real heavies like the flowering stems of cardoon, *Cynara cardunculus*, need chestnut posts and telephone cables (or a heavy grade of tarred string) for support.

Dead-heading of spent blooms continues right through the summer and into autumn. Conscientiously pursued, it makes all the difference to a border's appearance as the season progresses. Never dead-head to leave a projecting piece of stem. Cut back almost flush with the base of a leaf or pair of leaves.

With some flowers you dead-head in the expectation of a second crop to follow; for instance *Salvia* 'Superba' (more persistent than any of the dwarf cultivars), early flowering phloxes and heleniums, *Anthemis tinctoria*. When a low plant like *Viola cornuta*, *Geranium sanguineum*, giant chives (*Allium*) or *Alchemilla mollis* looks spent and tatty, cut it all to the ground, give it a dose of fertilizer and water heavily.

In other cases, and with shrubs like summer flowering buddleias, the Jerusalem sage (*Phlomis fruticosa*) and *Senecio* 'Sunshine', the dead-heading is a mere tidying up procedure.

Meantime the process of rejuvenating certain areas in the border can go right into late August or early September with the introduction of chrysanthemum and michaelmas daisy plants.

The time has come to consider the kinds of plants suitable for mixed borders in greater detail.

Shrubs

Two kinds of shrubs can be distinguished for our purpose. There are those which build up a permanent framework and comprise backbone elements. They develop a structure and give body to a planting which can be appreciated and enjoyed in winter as well as summer.

Second, there are those whose growth we restrict by hard pruning every year and which therefore develop little more personality than does a herbaceous plant. That, in its peak season, can be considerable but in winter it is nothing. These are shrubs that we grow for their late summer flowers or for foliage effect. I'll take the first group first.

STRUCTURAL SHRUBS

Most such flower on the wood they made in the previous year and they do so in the following spring; at latest, as with *Philadelphus*, by mid-July. The vast majority of flowering shrubs belong to spring. If our border aims, as it probably will do, at a summer season, such shrubs will be a drug on the market. They will be so many lumps of greenery.

This is not to say that a mixed border specialising in an April-May season could not be made. The foliage of many hostas is at its freshest then. Perennials with an early flowering season would be included near the border's margin, for most such are short-stemmed. There would be dicentras and early primulas; doronicums, omphalodes and brunneras. Many such plants are tolerant of shade, so they could run into the shrub plantings. There would be globe flowers, the double white *Ranunculus aconitifolius* as well as other double buttercups. Forget-me-nots could be allowed to self-sow and there would be the big white violet, *Viola cucullata* as well as smaller drift-forming kinds like the yellow *V. biflora* and the purple *V. labradorica* which also has purple leaves and shows up so well with that low-growing evergreen shrub *Euonymus fortunei* 'Green-'n-Gold'. Given reasonable moisture, ferns could run in and out of the shrubs, particularly the shuttlecock, *Matteuccia struthiopteris*; the sensitive, *Onoclea sensibilis*, and the oak, *Gymnocarpium dryopteris*, all of remarkable freshness in the early part of their season.

There would be little scope for annuals, perhaps, but of biennials the lime green, parsley-like inflorescences and conspicuous bracts of *Smyrnium perfoliatum* would be particularly at home as also the various strains of honesty, *Lunaria annua*, of which the pure white form shows up best beneath shrub shade.

Bulbs would be there in force, though I should tend to avoid the largest and most lumpish tulips and daffodils. The latters' leaves die off particularly obtrusively in May. Erythroniums would be absolutely right as also the rhizomatous anemones such as *Anemone apennina*. Once established, *Cyclamen repandum* can make a splendid colony beneath shrubs.

All this would make an exciting exercise and to get the balance right I think you should actually lay emphasis on the herbs and bulbs and not yield to the temptation of allowing azaleas and other rhododendrons (assuming that your soil is acid enough to grow them), camellias, viburnums, corylopsis, barberries, spiraeas and the rest of them become too dominant. Remember that spring-flowering herbs, bulbs and the plants like hostas, rodgersias and ferns grown for their foliage, have a much better chance to develop well among and, even more so, underneath deciduous shrubs, which cast little shade until late May, than among evergreens.

An early-season mixed border such as this would carry little interest beyond May. A garden needs to be fairly large for the owners to be prepared to turn their backs on a major feature from June onwards, just when we expect to enjoy living in the open most. It is short-sighted to allow ourselves to be dominated by the spring garden. A rule of thumb that I have found to work well for me is to concentrate, in my planning, on the summer and autumn scene. Spring, with all the freshness of foliage which turns the whole countryside into something as beguiling as any garden, has a way of looking after itself.

So I will return to my original concept of a mixed border that concentrates on the mid-June to mid-August period, but encourages foretastes and aftermaths insofar as these do not detract from the main season.

Viburnum opulus 'Compactum', for instance, gets in on the basis of flowering prettily with white lacecaps in May, but more importantly, of already ripening its clusters of gleaming red berries in August and these hang on for several months without attracting the birds (don't ask me why). This is a less voluminous version of our native guelder rose, but it does need quite careful pruning both to reduce its bulk and to promote a steady flow of flowers and fruit without these becoming a biennial feature with no contribution in the off years. Come the winter, when your shrub is naked and can be properly seen, remove some of the most heavily fruited branches and leave those that have quite a lot of young wood on them and will flower and fruit for you on this in the next season.

Mahonia 'Undulata' is a shrub that I give space to, even though it flowers in April. Its glossy, wavy-margined leaves are particularly smart, and they change to sumptuous purple in the cold winter's weather. Even so, it must not occupy as much space as it would like, and I cut it hard back into old wood every fifth spring.

Weigela florida 'Variegata' is not a wonderful shrub, structurally, however well you prune it, and its flowering season – a mass of scented, pale pink trumpets – in May, is well outside our requirements. But its foliage, first green and white, then green and yellow, is a meal in itself and makes a wonderful background to bronze or red flowers, as it might be heleniums or dahlias.

The Mount Etna broom, *Genista aetnensis*, is a case of its own. It is the longest lived of all the brooms (mine is now 35 years old and still going strong) and it eventually becomes a small tree, 15 or more feet high, but because its growth is so light and airy, making virtually no foliage, it never becomes overbearing. So much light penetrates its branches that you can plant underneath with other summer flowerers. Its own season, when it is a fountain of tiny yellow, scented blossom, is July-August.

Of the structural shrubs that you plant in a mixed border, I should warn that they are often slow growing in youth (structure takes time to build up) compared with their flimsy annual, biennial or herbaceous perennial neighbours. The latter can easily shade them out, in these early years, and this requires preventative vigilance on your part.

SHRUBS FOR SUMMER–AUTUMN FLOWERING OR FOR FOLIAGE EFFECT

These shrubs, in the main, make their display, whether of flowers or of foliage, on young shoots of the current season's growth. They therefore lend themselves to a hard annual cutting back. This, it will be observed, is the same treatment as we give to hardy perennials, the only difference being that in the one case we cut to the ground, in the other to a stool, stump or lowish framework. The annual habit of growth, in each case, is very similar, which makes this type of shrub particularly well suited to the company of perennials. Their needs are the same.

Cultivars of the butterfly bush, *Buddleia davidii*, are the best known example. Of the shrub *Hypericum*, 'Hidcote' is familiar with its flat saucers of yellow flowers. Richer coloured and more deeply cupped is 'Rowallane', but it is slightly less hardy. The summer flowering tamarisk, *Tamarix ramosissima* (better known as *T. pentandra*), produces a haze of pink spikelets in a gauze of pale green foliage. You can cut it back in winter to a 2 or 3 foot stump. It looks well, in its season, behind *Verbena bonariensis* or next to the tall white *Cimicifuga racemosa*.

The scented Spanish broom, *Spartium junceum*, flowers in yellows spikelets at the tips of its young shoots, and looks well with something white, as it might be a *Philadelphus* or rose 'Iceberg'. Many fuchsias are remarkably hardy, but mostly respond best to being cut to the ground each early spring. The red and purple 'Mrs Popple' looks well, at 3 feet, with the somewhat taller, pale pink *Abelia × grandiflora*. Both have a long season.

Blue-flowered shrubs are all too rare but such are the hardy plumbago *Ceratostigma willmottianum* (another good partner for red fuchsias), *Caryopteris × clandonensis*, of which the most intensively coloured clones are 'Ferndown', 'Kew Blue' and 'Heavenly Blue'; and *Perovskia atriplicifolia*, with branching panicles of sage-like flowers on upright 3 to 4 foot stems.

Romneya, the Californian tree poppy, responds to being cut absolutely to ground level in winter, at which time it can take turns with a dazzling display of winter aconites (*Eranthis*) and *Crocus tommasinianus* (with variations at your pleasure). Floppy white, yellow-stamened poppies are borne at 6 foot in July-August above grey foliage. This plant spreads by suckering and will take up quite a lot of space. So does and will *Sambucus canadensis* 'Maxima', an elder that flowers on its young wood with enormous corymbs, a foot or more across.

Among hydrangeas, the ultra-hardy kinds that flower on their young shoots and respond to a hard winter cut back, are all white. *Hydrangea paniculata* has a cone-shaped inflorescence, and is most popular in the cultivar 'Grandiflora', wherein the florets are all of the large, sterile kind and make a heavy head. It fades to pink. More elegant are 'Tardiva' and 'Floribunda' (the difference between them eludes me), in which the large sterile florets are interspersed with a fuzz of tiny fertile ones. In *H. arborescens* 'Grandiflora' (another heavy-headed but excellent clone) and *H. a. discolor* 'Sterilis', the inflorescence is globular. These look smashing with border phloxes, cultivars of *Phlox paniculata*, and both will put up with quite a bit of shade. Another good partner for the July-flowering 'Sterilis' is the spiky yellow loosestrife, *Lysimachia punctata*.

Other hydrangeas, whether lacecaps or hortensias (flat-headed or bun-shaped) are first rate mixed border ingredients and they are generally coloured, but their pruning is not of the cutting back type. In March you should remove 3 to 4-year-old branches that have become weakened by flowering, either completely, right back to ground level (a narrow-bladed saw helps you to get really low among a forest of stems) or back to a strong, unbranched young shoot if such occurs in its lower regions. In this way you thin out and let light into a bush, which itself encourages the production of new growth in the next season and renews the entire bush over a period of four years or so. Generous feeding in spring should go with this treatment.

Hydrangeas look well in groups and, being deciduous, lend themselves to underplanting with early bulbs. One of the most effective in a mixed border setting is 'Preziosa' (derived from *H. serrata*) with small bun heads of sterile florets that start pale pink but gradually change to deep ruby red (purple, on acid soil). The leaves and young stems are attractively flushed red. It has a long season because new flower heads keep developing. This is also a main asset in 'Générale Vicomtesse de Vibraye', a hortensia which is probably at its most alluring on acid soil, when the colouring is light blue. It is one of the hardiest.

Quite different are the large shrubs with felted leaves made by *H. sargentiana* and *H. villosa*. Both are winter hardy but subject to serious damage by spring frosts on their young shoots. They also need wind shelter to prevent bruising of their large leaves in summer. In *H. sargentiana* these may, in a shady situation, be 15 inches long by 9 inches across. The lacecap flower heads with a ring of sterile florets surrounding a platform of tiny fertile flowers, are pale mauve. The colouring is a rich shade of lilac in the sterile florets of *H. villosa*, while the central flowers are blue. In its August season this is the most beautiful flower in my garden. There is a dense carpet beneath it of *Saxifraga × geum*, whose mist of tiny blush flowers appears in May.

The best known and perhaps the showiest *Indigofera* is *I. heterantha*, with axillary spikelets of deep rosy mauve pea flowers. You can keep this to a low framework or cut it to the ground, if you prefer, in which case it will not exceed 3 to 4 foot.

There are some rather more substantial late flowering shrubs that do not demand hard pruning. Most are white-flowered, which is curious. Some useful privet species come into this category, in particular the August-September *Ligustrum quihoui*, which is peculiarly elegant with narrow leaves and long sprays of blossom. Pruning consists of removing flowered shoots in winter, leaving the unflowered wands intact. *Ligustrum × vicaryi* is July-flowering and also carries handsome crops of black berries. Its evergreen leaves are lime green. Again, remove flowered and fruited branches to prune.

Eucryphias have white summer flowers with many stamens. *Eucryphia glutinosa* is the hardiest, a deciduous shrub, colouring well in the autumn. 'Nymansay' will make a tree in time but can be kept to a narrow spire, with a little help. Its bold flowers open in August and are a workshop for bees. It will tolerate some lime, which *E. glutinosa* does not.

Hoheria glabrata and *H. lyallii* are similar and often muddled, which doesn't really matter. Both are fast growing shrubs in the mallow family with heart-shaped leaves and masses of white, scented blossom (not unlike a cherry's in general effect) in July.

The great merit of foliage shrubs in a mixed border is the tremendous value they give – year-round in some cases. My biggest feature would be a tree. Dickson's golden elm (*Ulmus* 'Dicksonii', of uncertain parentage), with its bright lime green colouring, makes a yellow impression which lasts the season through. It looks all the better for clipping (done every other year) because the leaves on the young shoots rise vertically in two ranks and overlap like feathers. A pale silver-grey willow in front makes a telling contrast: our native white willow *Salix alba* in a less vigorous but whiter form, 'Argentea'. It receives an annual pollarding in winter. To complete the mixed border image, I have established a handsome parasite on its roots (from a lump of soil containing its own roots), *Lathraea clandestina*. Entirely leafless, its bright purple, hooded flowers appear in dense clusters just above ground level in March and continue flowering till May. There are also scented violets, some pink, some purple, beneath these shrubs.

It is a holly, *Ilex × altaclerensis* 'Golden King', filling the back corner of my mixed border, that gives greatest year-round pleasure. It is almost prickle-free (which makes a lot of difference when you're grubbing about for weeds), with a golden leaf margin. It berries freely almost every year. Although slow growing it is the better for clipping over by hand every 5 or 6 years, so as to retain a dense habit.

Lonicera nitida 'Baggesen's Gold' I clip every year in February, just as growth is starting up. It looks awful at first but soon takes on a more relaxed appearance and if you don't do this the plant soon becomes scrawny. Its yellow-green colouring looks well in conjunction with *Cotinus coggygria* in its purple (but greenish purple, not purple purple) form, 'Purpurea', which also makes masses of purplish 'smoke' on the inflorescence. The deep 'Notcutt's Variety' and the even richer 'Royal Purple' do not do this.

If you want 'Purpurea' to flower, prune selectively in winter, leaving those young shoots you wish to flower unpruned. If pruning entirely for foliage effect, as with 'Royal Purple', you can shorten the shoots all over. However, this weakens the shrub if done severely every year, so every other is generally the best compromise. A purple cotinus behind a deep pink phlox looks good in sunshine, or with the lime green blossom of *Alchemilla mollis* in front of it. Another telling combination is of the purple continus planted with the brilliantly glaucous foliage of *Eucalyptus gunnii*, itself stooled (i.e. cut back to a low stump) every or every other year. This promotes the disc-like juvenile foliage, which is the brightest and prettiest.

Another purple-leaved shrub (dusky mauve, really, with glaucous hints) that combines well with the eucalyptus is *Rosa glauca* (*R. rubrifolia*) grown entirely for foliage. To this end you cut back annually. You should also grow a plant more naturally for its modest but engaging flowers and its clusters of showy hips. From these you will find yourself the owner of self-sown seedlings, which you can then assemble into a group, planted 2 or 3 feet apart, and give them the foliage treatment.

Among the most silvery of grey-leaved shrubs is *Santolina pinnata neapolitana*, paler, with a longer leaf and more open-textured than the better known lavender cotton. Flowering is to the detriment of a foliage shrub like this. You prevent it and also promote a close-textured habit by cutting back to a low, woody stump each spring; spring, not winter, in cases like this where there is an element of doubt about hardiness. Even hardier, however, yet fulfilling the same function, a mound of grey at the 18 inch level, is *Helichrysum splendidum*. This is a stiffer shrub. It looks well in front of the feathery-textured conifer, *Chamaecyparis thyoides* 'Ericoides', which is sea green in summer, purple in winter.

Excellent grey value also from the comb leaves of *Artemisia* 'Powis Castle', 2 foot tall and of a spreading habit. It does not worry you by flowering and looking patchy. By the same token it needs less pruning. *Senecio cineraria* (*Cineraria maritima*) demands a hard spring cut-back. It has felted, pinnate leaves, whitest in 'White Diamond', most cut in 'Ramparts'. If you have a group of these you can interplant them with dwarf tulips, which will do their stuff while the shrub is in its reduced, cut-back phase. All this at the border's margin, as we're talking in terms of 12 to 18 inch tall plants.

The most beautiful of all foliage plants that you can grow as hardy (if you're careful) is the South African *Melianthus major*, with sizeable, wax-smooth pinnate leaves, glaucous and with sharply toothed margins that cast shadows on the leaf surface when the sun is low. Although a shrub, you treat it as a herbaceous perennial, cutting its old stems (whether live or dead) down in spring. Meantime, in winter, you should pack fern fronds between them and cover the crowns, as a protection. Once established, the roots go deep, the shoots also appearing from quite deep down in spring, and you'll never lose it.

A Japanese maple is unlikely to be good material for a mixed border since it grows too slowly in the early years to compete with lush neighbours; otherwise I would certainly include *Acer japonicum* 'Aureum'. But the same colouring can be had on the large pinnate leaves of the golden cut-leaved elder, *Sambucus racemosa* 'Plumosa Aurea' and this, cut down to stumps in winter, will make 4 feet of growth in a season. Like many golden leaved plants it tends to scorch in hot sunlight, especially if the soil is dry. Dense shade, on the other hand, will result in too green a colouring. Part shade is the right compromise.

There are a few trees or shrubs from which you can obtain enormous leaves by dint of cutting them to the ground each winter and then allowing only a few shoots per plant to develop. This creates a really exotic effect. Three of the best for this are *Paulownia tomentosa*, with big heart leaves (you can raise it from seed), *Ailanthus glandulosa*, the tree of heaven, with pinnate leaves and *Rhus glabra* 'Laciniata' (better than *R. typhina*), also pinnate, from a naturally suckering shrub. The last has bright autumn colour. Don't start hacking at these too hard until they've had a year or two to establish strongly. I should like to see the paulownia grouped with giant annual sunflowers (*Helianthus*).

CLIMBERS

Climbers have two particular values in a mixed border. They can prolong or add another dimension to a shrub's season by being allowed to grow through or over it; or they may be trained as vertical features on their own supports. Either way they take up little or no border space; no special sites have to be allowed for them and so, to the plantsman, they are a bonus that can be fitted in without thereby excluding something else.

You can train an ivy up a pole. Rising above a sea of lesser plants it will make a conspicuous and important feature. I have grown *Hedera canariensis* 'Variegata' on a chestnut pole for many years. Having quickly reached the top, its young shoots explored the air like feelers reaching towards outer space. Every year, I trim it hard back to the pole. This, at the end of the first 8 or 10 years, rotted, the weak spot being, as usual, at ground level. You cannot take ivy off a pole so I cut it down and put a new pole in (about 10ft. long). The ivy didn't take long to cover its new support. This has never given way again and I suspect that the ivy now supports the pole.

Clematis make a good vertical feature on a pole, too. I find this a preferable support to a tripod. It takes up less room and the clematis hides it more efficiently. Clematis flowering from late June or early July onwards, on their young wood, are the most suitable. My most faithful example has been a *C.* × *jackmanii* 'Superba', planted 25 years ago. I cut it down to the ground every year, then tie in its young shoots with tarred string (soft string is tweaked off by sparrows for nesting material) as they rise. A step ladder is needed for the last ties. A column of purple blossom is the result and looks good behind a 6 to 7 foot group of the yellow *Senecio doria*, which is rather like a giant ragwort but with plain, undivided leaves.

Clematis can be used throughout a mixed border to liven up the shrubs. Wherever you see a shrub looking a bit dull, ask yourself which clematis would look well growing with it. You must take care to match the vigour of one with the other so that the clematis does not overwhelm its host. If the weight and volume of a clematis seems to be too much for its supporter, you can knock a pole in and train some of the clematis up that, the rest over the shrub.

Climbing honeysuckles can be treated in the same way. I have *Lonicera* × *americana* on a pole devoted to it alone. On other occasions I find wild honeysuckle seeding into my borders and sometimes in a place where I can leave it; for instance, growing up *Eucryphia* 'Nymansay'. The honeysuckle growth has to be curbed every few years or it would strangle its host but it flowers earlier than the eucryphia and thus prolongs its season. Another good self-choice was over a clump of female skimmias. These look dull in June-July, when the honeysuckle is in bloom. Later, the berries of the one vie with the berries of the other, both in red clusters.

On a strong tree/shrub you can grow a Virginia creeper, *Parthenocissus quinquifolia*, or, less vigorous, *P. henryana*. But even better in some cases would be *P. inserta*, which is a tendril climber without adhesive discs (which are unnecessary in the circumstances). I grow this through the gaunt, double white lilac, *Syringa* 'Mme Lemoine'. So far the lilac, whose root system is terrific, has the upper hand. I should have planted the climber at some distance from the lilac's trunk and trained it into some outer branches up a strand of string. This policy also works well with clematis, when it is dark, dry and rooty close to its host's trunk.

The herbaceous perennial species of pea have a place in your border. Gertrude Jekyll used to train the white-flowered form of *Lathyrus latifolius* to cover up the withering remains of *Gypsophila paniculata* in late summer. The bricky red *L. rotundifolius* could be used likewise. *Lathyrus grandiflorus* is the everlasting pea, not everlasting *sweet* pea, as you so often hear; none of these perennial peas has any scent. It has sizeable magenta flowers and looks particularly well, I think, in a large specimen of purple leaved barberry (*Berberis* × *ottawensis* 'Purpurea', for instance) or a not so much pruned, purple *Cotinus coggygria*. But its tuberous root system is invasive and you may sometimes need to read the riot act. This may also be the case with the flame nasturtium, *Tropaeolum speciosum*, which you will consider a weed if you live in the northwest of Scotland but a cherished prize in southeast England. It can do well in the drier southeast if the soil is not alkaline. The flowers, throughout the summer and early autumn, are a very special shade of intense red. It looks particularly well over azaleas and other rhododendrons, out of their own season. The tuberous roots are great travellers and hard to catch, so this is a plant not freely available.

Nasturtiums are tropaeolums (*T. majus*) and they are to our purpose, although you must vigilantly prevent their self-sown seedlings from overpowering smaller plants. It looks marvellous to see trails of red nasturtiums flinging themselves over a mauve mound of *Aster sedifolius* (*A. acris*), for instance or into the cream plumes of *Artemisia lactiflora*. Or, for that matter, up the hedge that forms the background to your border. Nasturtiums do need a little attention, at times. They dislike drought and they are often attacked by black aphids and by cabbage white (the Large White) caterpillars.

ROSES

To treat roses separately is merely to acknowledge that they are a particularly important class of shrub. As all roses are shrubs, we are indulging in tautology when we speak of shrub roses. The roses we mean to include under this title are those that do not readily lend themselves to bedding. They do not conform to the herd instict but behave more as individuals. Often they are individually large plants, and there is then little incentive to grouping them.

As individuals, they are still most often lacking in style. The massive legs and hostile thorns are still in evidence. This is where their inclusion in a mixed border can have such an enormous advantage. If you grow blue and white *Campanula persicifolia* through the centre of a congenitally scrawny 'Crested Moss' rose, not only will they flower delightfully together but the rose's spindly legs will vanish from sight.

Bulbs will achieve the same object. For instance, underneath the skirts of a dwarfish rose 'The Fairy' suitable for a border's margin, you can grow the 15 inch tall Chinese chives, *Allium tuberosum*, which flowers in late summer. Its white, green-centred umbels will push through the rose and appear among the latter's pink blooms.

If the stiffness of a rose is on a large scale, as it would be in 'Queen Elizabeth' or 'Chinatown', grow a clematis like 'Perle d'Azur' through it. A large specimen of *Rosa moyesii* could take the weight of a *Clematis flammula*, and the frothy white blossom of the one would coincide with the ripening red hips of the other.

Many roses will have the advantage, in your border, of a double season of interest; either flowers followed by fruits as in *R. moyesii*, *R. setipoda* and the Rugosa roses, or two crops of flowers. 'Florence May Morse' is my favourite in that respect, as it is such an excellent clear shade of red, and this is a colour none too easy to find in shrubs and hardy perennials. Another favourite repeat bloomer with me is 'Perle d'Or', which has miniature tea rose flowers, apricot, shading to off-white at the margins, on a 5 foot shrub. Its second crop tends to be particularly well scented on the air, thanks, most probably, to the moisture-laden air of early autumn.

Roses are not nearly so subject to their usual range of diseases – rust, black spot, mildew and the like – in a mixed community. But you will be queering your own pitch if you start massing roses in a mixed border. That would defeat the object of the exercise.

As with other shrubs, it will be wise to avoid most of those roses which contribute but the one flowering, in June, and have nothing further to offer, unless you are clever enough to substitute a climber going through them which will compensate with plenty of later blossom yet without destroying its host's sound health.

Hardy perennials

Don't let the hardy plants be squeezed out by the shrubs. They are the great providers of splodges of bright colour (and I include white as such) in high summer. In this role there is nothing among the shrubs to touch them.

Before discussing some of the principals, let me say something about stature. In order to accommodate them to small gardens and also to cut out the effort of providing support, plant breeders have reduced the height of many plants which naturally grow quite tall. The trouble with these induced dwarfs is that most of them have a rather tight, bunched up appearance. Few inherit the grace of their tall antecedents. On the whole, then, I would say that where short plants are called for it is best (and quite simple) to use those that are naturally low growing, like *Crepis incana*, *Carlina acaulis*, *Epilobium glabellum*, *Sedum spectabile* (and most other sedums), violas, the lower cranesbills, diascias and hostas. And it would be my same recommendation for the annuals and bedding plants.

Of many campanulas for a mixed border, the queen, perhaps, is *Campanula lactiflora* but, at 7 foot or so and requiring support, it can grow inordinately tall. The tiny 'Pouffe', on the other hand, is one of those induced dwarfs of which I have just been writing. The answer is 'Prichard's Variety'. This grows about 3 feet tall and is a darker, more definite shade of campanula blue than some of the rather milky mauves.

There is nothing to touch delphiniums, but they do leave rather a gap. Treating them as short-lived perennials to be renewed fairly frequently from seed, you can afford to cut them right down after flowering (a slightly weakening operation) and wait for new growth to give you a second crop of flowers in September. Secondary growth in delphiniums will always be attacked by mildew but you can anticipate by watering your plants with Benlate (benomyl) when the young shoots appear. New delphinium seed strains are constantly appearing. I have had good results with 'Blue Fountain', said to be a mere 2¼ feet tall, but in their second year, at any rate, they will run up to 5 feet or more. I don't like them too short anyway.

Lupins are a nuisance in most mixed borders because they flower early and look a wreck, however you treat them, from mid or late June onwards. If you must grow them (and I certainly must), treat them as biennials. Raise a new batch from seed each spring, grow them on in a spare plot till autumn planting out time. Then, throw them out at midsummer and replace with an annual raised from seed sown in May. (See illustrations pp. 6–7.)

Oriental poppies (from *Papaver orientale* and its relatives) provide a marvellous foretaste of summer and can be included in a July border without weakening the main impact. They do not resent being cut to the ground after flowering, which enables you to plant very close to their roots with bedding plants such as dahlias or cannas. The most upstanding poppy, generally requiring no support, is *P. bracteatum* 'Goliath', which grows 4 foot tall and carries enormous blood red blooms of the greatest delicacy in texture.

I nowadays exclude peonies (*Paeonia lactiflora* and *P. officinalis* cultivars) from my borders, because their season is so short and they become passengers from late June which you cannot readily mask. However, you could try growing a plant of *Lathyrus latifolius* (see p. 30) or of *Clematis flammula* (with masses of scented white blossom in August-September) behind a peony group and allow the climber to take over in the latter part of the season. Otherwise I recommend growing peonies in a picking plot.

Of the michaelmas daisy tribe, most have too late and short a season to be useful. Such are the cultivars of *Aster novae-angliae* and *A. novi-belgii*. By far the most rewarding is the lavender coloured *A.* × *frikartii* 'Moench', which starts flowering in early August and carries on for two months. Growing $2\frac{1}{2}$ to 3 feet tall, it is self-supporting after the first year and its flowers are quite large as asters go. I like it with a yellow *Heliopsis* (one of the perennial sunflowers) such as 'Golden Plume' ($3\frac{1}{2}$ feet).

Shasta daisies, *Chrysanthemum maximum*, tend to be a somewhat baleful and corpse-like white, with heavy green foliage that doesn't help any. The single-flowered kinds have the great merit of a yellow central disc, which gives colour relief. My own favourite is 'Everest' (4 foot) which has the largest single flowers, especially if you replant with small pieces every other year. Size does not lead to grossness, here.

Border phloxes – *Phlox paniculata* and *P. maculata* cultivars – are a marvellous standby in July and August on heavy, moisture-retaining soils. Healthy stock, free of eelworm (nematode) infection is paramount. For this reason I seldom buy a plant from a nursery, preferring to beg a piece from a friend's garden in which I can see that the plants have nothing wrong with them. When infected by eelworm, the leaves of phlox become puckered and many of them drawn out to fine threads. Once seen, never forgotten. Don't bother about the names of phloxes. Be guided by

the colours you like and the robustness with which they grow. Phloxes are greedy and thirsty. They need replanting in improved soil every fourth year. If you try switching positions with them you'll find they get all mixed up, as pieces of root left behind make new plants.

The most effective *Monarda*, the bee balm, smelling of lemons, is 'Cambridge Scarlet', which is really a good crimson red and not scarlet. It flowers in July and there's nothing to compare with a healthy quilt of it then. Subject to mildew, however, and to dying out in winter. 'Cobham Beauty' is nice, with pink flowers and purple bracts. A top dressing with old potting soil, when the young shoots are a couple of inches high in spring, helps to prevent the colony from starving itself out.

The yellow-flowered yarrows have a strong personality in a border, especially *Achillea filipendulina* 'Gold Plate' (5 feet) and 'Coronation Gold' (3 feet). They carry table-top corymbs of mustard yellow flowers in July, gradually losing freshness just as made up English mustard does when it is kept too long. Use with restraint. At $2\frac{1}{2}$ foot *A.* 'Moonshine' is a paler but still bright yellow, set off by silvery foliage. Old colonies tend to stop flowering and become foliage plants only. Prettiest of the lot is the pale lemon yellow, 2 foot *A.* × *taygetea*, but it is less robust thatn the others and not always winter hardy; it is worth a bit of trouble, however. The white forms of *A. ptarmica* are of secondary value, except for cutting. Their running habit with slender white rhizomes is a great nuisance.

Opposite: *Viola cornuta* 'Alba', *Rosa pimpinellifolia* 'William III', *Hosta sieboldiana* 'Elegans' and *Alchemilla mollis*.
Above: Foliage contrast with hosta and climbing golden hop (supported).
Below: Suitable for shade – hosta and fern with double pink campion (*Melandrium rubrum* 'Flore Pleno').

Except in rather moist woodland settings, I have gone off the majority of astilbes, as they flower for too short a time (a fortnight). True the inflorescence never looks ugly after flowering but they are among the first plants to look unhappy when water is short. Exceptionally, the 3½ foot *Astilbe taquetii* has a long season, starting rather late; beautiful foliage, rather narrow panicles of a singularly bright mauve. Lovely contrasted with the heads of pink hortensia hydrangeas. It seeds itself in a most agreeable manner so that you find outliers from your main colony.

Hemerocallis, the day lilies, have attained enormous popularity and you need to be careful in your selection. Visit the RHS trial at Wisley in July. Some with beautiful blooms are not sufficiently free with them at any one time. It is also a good idea to stand back from a clump and see how well it shows up in the distance. Many day lily colours are too lurid or muddy to be seen except at close quarters. Remember that the plant itself is far from neat. 'Corky' (yellow) and 'Golden Chimes' (bronze and yellow) are exceptionally prolific though individual flowers are small. These are only 2½ feet tall. So is *H. flava*, the earliest to flower (early June) and the sweetest scented. This is clear yellow, but the earliness of its season is a disadvantage. If you get bored with its foliage, cut it right down after flowering. It will soon grow again and remain fresh until autumn 'Marion Vaughn' is a luminous, large flowered pale yellow for late July and August. Hemerocallis lend themselves to interplanting with narcissi and jonquils.

The hostas are even more popular than the day lilies. Although particularly suited to shade, they will often put up a remarkable performance when hot and dry. In the main they must be considered as foliage plants, particularly suited to shrubbery margins in the early part of their season. For later effect, *Hosta ventricosa* 'Variegata' ('Aureo-Marginata' in the States) not only retains a lively creamy yellow margin to its broad heart leaves but flowers abundantly, to great effect with spires of lavender bells. That is in July, which is also the flowering season of *H. lancifolia* (running through August) with flared trumpet flowers at 15 inches and 'Tall Boy', with similar flowers but upstanding to 4 or 5 feet.

A healthy colony of *H. crispula* (all hostas are subject to virus disease) looks even smarter, with its broad white leaf margin, than the more robust and frequently seen 'Thomas Hogg'. Both need shade to protect the white from sun scorch. They show up well beneath a *Fatsia japonica* whose lower branches have been removed. Here also you could grow ferns for leaf contrast and interplant with snowdrops for early interest. This is the essence of mixed border gardening. Another hosta for this setting would be *H. undulata*, of petite habit and variegated in streaks throughout the leaves which have an elegant twist on them.

The glaucous-leaved hostas need more sun to bring out their blue colouring. *H. sieboldiana* 'Elegans' is one of the best known and largest-leaved with a rippling texture. Some of the modern hybrids (like 'Buckshaw Blue') are so blue as scarcely to look real. They are pristine in spring and early summer and tend to look tired from July onwards. *Hosta plantaginea* is then at its best, however, its yellow-green foliage retaining a remarkable freshness until September. The pick of the hybrids from this is 'Royal Standard' (far better than 'Honey Bells') with night-scented white trumpets in late summer.

Blue-leaved hostas look uncommonly well close to another genus of moisture-loving foliage plants, *Rodgersia*. The most striking is *R. pinnata* 'Superba', whose bold, pinnate leaves are purple in May. It flowers freely and the inflorescence is a pink panicle, in late June, gradually darkening as it ages to dusky red in autumn. Thus its season of beauty is five months long. *Rodgersia podophylla* has leaflets like a webbed foot. They take on rosy autumnal colouring from midsummer onwards but can scorch under stress.

Sedums, by contrast, are great drought resisters. 'Autumn Joy' is a mainstay in every garden. You do not want to be overloaded with it in a summer border, but even then its green broccoli-like heads of buds make a distinct impression. The flowers are pale dusky pink in late August, gradually deepening to a warm autumnal red; finally brown and holding their shape throughout the winter. *Sedum spectabile* is the one that butterflies go for in a big way and it is pure pink, more intense in 'Brilliant'. This is only a foot tall, against 'Autumn Joy's' 18 inches. *S. spectabile* flowers in August with a moderately brief season. *Sedum maximum* 'Atropurpureum' is a rather coarse 2 foot plant with deep purple leaves, for which it is grown, and dusky flowers. Not an easy plant to place effectively, it is shown up well when interplanted with the grey foliage of *Senecio cineraria* (see p. 27).

Sedum 'Ruby Glow' is nearly prostrate and can be overplanted with bulbs. *Allium christophii* is a suitable choice as its big globes, in flower in June, continue to look handsome when dying, at which time, in August-September, the sedum is in its stride, with purplish red flowers. 'Vera Jameson' is another purple-leaved sedum neater than the others, about a foot tall.

The vast genus *Salvia* (the sages) includes tender and hardy plants, shrubs, annuals and biennials. *S. guaranitica* starts flowering in August and is deep blue, contrasting well with yellow or with the orange of *Tithonia rotundifolia* 'Torch' (an annual). The sage grows 3 foot tall and is tuberous rooted, not reliably hardy. Lift at least one root each autumn to overwinter under glass. Easily raised from spring cuttings from young shoots. It is safest to

overwinter a clump of *Salvia uliginosa* in the same way. It makes a forest of 5 foot shoots bearing short spikes of clear, rather light blue flowers. Not a common colour in its August season.

Salvia nemorosa 'Superba' is the pick of the hardy perennials, a fairly massive plant to $3\frac{1}{2}$ foot (safer with some support) and carrying a mass of blue purple flower spikes in which the bracts are reddish purple. A lovely contrast to the scarlet domes of *Lychnis chalcedonica* (but see p. 10) in July. There are some good dwarf earlier flowering kinds (with more being developed in Germany) but they do not have the staying power of 'Superba' with its capacity for producing a second crop in September. 'East Friesland' is a fine purple dwarf, at 18 inches, and makes a delightful partner for the flat heads of the pale yellow *Achillea* × *taygetea*.

In the mixed border context, *Lychnis coronaria* should not be omitted. It has grey, felted leaves and stems which highlight its brilliant magenta disc flowers from early July to late August. These harmonise well with the dusky pink and grey-green tones of *Fuchsia magellanica* 'Versicolor', while the biennial or at least monocarpic *Eryngium giganteum*, a 3 foot sea holly with ghost pale bracts and sea green flowers, would make up an excellent trio. The eryngium self-sows and the lychnis must be depended upon to do the same, as it exhausts itself after two years' flowering. So your colonies of each will continually be jostling for supremacy.

Opposite: Globe flower (*Trollius* 'Canary Bird') and *Ranunculus aconitifolius* 'Flore Pleno', overhung in shady border by *Hydrangea* 'Quadricolor'. Above: Accent on yellow, with kniphofia backed by golden-variegated dogwood. Below: Yellow and white border, with Spanish broom, rose 'Iceberg' and *Oenothera missouriensis* in foreground.

I have not yet mentioned *Iris* and, indeed, the bearded kinds are not at all good as mixed border plants. It isn't simply because they flower too early and for too short a season but because their leaves look tired and usually spotted from late June onwards and there is no way of masking or interplanting them. They need to have the sun beating on their rhizomes. In a large border you can accommodate a few of the *I. sibirica* and *I. spuria* types and hope that they will not be too noticeable after their faded flower heads have been removed.

Neither have I found perennial *Dianthus* to be very satisfactory mixed border plants. Those with a long flowering season make the least comely plants. They have to be grown at the border's margin and there is no hope of disguising their shortcomings here. Pinks are happiest in dry walls or paving or in hot raised borders.

Geraniums, the hardy cranesbills, include a great many suitable members. Many are good in shade, so that they will flourish among and under the branches of shrubs. Such is the bright mauve-pink *Geranium endressii*, with a long season from May onwards. 'Wargrave' is a salmon pink cultivar and 'A.T. Johnson' a clearer, paler chalky pink but this last can be excessively vigorous, killing out its neighbours. A hard cut-back in mid-season is often a good plan. *Geranium psilostemon* often needs support at $3\frac{1}{2}$ feet but its intense magenta with a near black eye is most arresting. More valuable still, in the future, when a way of propagating it quickly and in quantity has been found, will be 'Ann Folkard', which has the same colouring but is a bushy plant no more than 2 foot tall and with a far more extended flowering season. There are a number of selected forms in meadow cranesbill, *G. pratense*, including a double 'blue' and a double purple ('Plenum Caeruleum' and 'Plenum Violaceum'). They all need support.

The magenta-flowered bloody cranesbill, *G. sanguineum*, is excellent at a border's margin. I have it in front of a pale grey *Santolina pinnata neapolitana* (see p. 27). There is a brilliant pink variant called 'Shepherd's Warning'. But the most rewarding marginal cranesbill of all, making a huge pool of magenta that spreads forwards and filters up into any thing a little taller than itself, is 'Russell Prichard'. It flowers from May to November and does not even require a mid-season trimming.

Geranium wallichianum 'Buxton's Blue' is very special, late in the season. It makes a rambling mat that reaches wide but dies right back to its crown in the winter. As it gets going late in spring, you can surround it with small bulbs like alliums (I have the pink, May-flowering *Allium murrayanum*), crocuses, scillas and chionodoxas. 'Buxton's Blue' starts flowering in July but its colour tends to be a slightly muddy mauve in hot weather. Later it becomes blue with a white centre and purple stamens, continuing into late October.

Mass rather than structure is by no means an invariable attribute in herbaceous perennials. Some make an exceedingly bold impact and will stand out, structurally, when seen right across a garden. They are often referred to as architectural plants.

Such is *Veratrum album*, a member of the lily family with pleated foliage not unlike a hosta's or a giant plantain's. The 5 foot inflorescence is composed of many white stars which are set along a branching panicle. It is extremely hardy, but uncommon because slow to propagate (from seed). Even if a nurseryman has the patience to bring a plant on to flowering size in five years or so, he is unlikely to command the price he deserves. Gardeners in Britain are extraordinarily mean about paying a realistic price for a hardy plant although they'll dig into their purses for a choice rhododendron without a murmur.

Acanthus are almost too easily propagated, from every piece of root, but they still need quite a bit of managing when being raised for sale. Their long, purplish spikes of hooded flowers have a sinister magnetism. *Acanthus balcanicus* (generally listed as *A. longifolius*), is one of the freest flowering and only 3 feet fall. *Acanthus spinosus* is taller and has handsomer leaves, while *A. mollis* has splendid soapy-textured foliage but is apt to be shy flowering.

The most desirable perennial eryngiums are often in short supply. Specially arresting is *E. × oliverianum*, 3 feet tall (rather floppy from the base) with steely blue stems and fairly large blue flower heads and bracts. Quite different, but a splendid mixed border ingredient if it will survive your winters (and it is not so very tender) is the Uraguayan species *E. decaisneanum* (*E. pandanifolium*). It has long, sea green, scimitar leaves. They are evergreen and spiny on the margins (don't poke your eye with them). The branching inflorescence is modest in colouring but rises to 8 foot in autumn and has an imposing presence.

Kniphofias, the red hot pokers, always stand out when in flower, though their season is often on the short side. *Cynara cardunculus*, the cardoon, has magnificent glaucous cut leaves followed by magnificent blue thistle heads – very close to the globe artichoke but more numerous, spinier, and up to 7 or 8 feet.

A plant does not have to be tall to be impressive, so long as its inflorescence has good bones. Such is *Carlina acaulis*, a foot-tall thistle with wide, bleached heads surrounded by a ruff of leaf-like bracts. In damp weather it remains doggedly closed, but when expanded in sunshine it is besieged by bees and butterflies.

Above: Tender bedding with perennial alstroemerias and shrubby
potentilla in Cottage Garden, Sissinghurst Castle.
Below: Late September free-for-all with annual *Linum grandiflorum*
'Rubrum' dominant.

Above: Tulip 'Orange Favourite' and self-sowing biennial white honesty give early interest.
Below: July mixture, including yellow *Asphodeline liburnica* which opens late afternoon.

Ornamental grasses and bamboos

In gardening terms, grasses are either clump formers or else they are spreaders and colonisers. Whatever their habit, but especially if they are colonisers, these grasses, however ornamental in themselves, look a mess when you pen them into a bed of their own. Their long narrow leaves need contrasts. Nothing easier than to give it them in a mixed border context. They contrast particularly well with dwarf conifers, especially those that flower above their evergreen partners. In my mixed border I have recently planted a *Pinus mugo* in front of the tall *Miscanthus sinensis* 'Silver Feather'. With such a length of leaf and stalk before you reach its flowers, at the 7 foot level, the grass needs something blocky by its side. I had thought of *Pittosporum tobira*, but that would not have been hardy enough, as I discovered when I lost it the previous winter! *Euphorbia wulfenii* would do the trick or *Daphne pontica*, if it didn't have to pant too much in the sun.

Miscanthus floridulus is another stately grass whose appearance becomes unnecessarily stemmy in its nether regions in the latter part of its growing season unless some sort of three-footer can fill in there. This grass grows to 9 feet or more (far less in the cooler north) between spring and autumn and, with its outward-curving leaves, looks like a foliar fountain. On a perfectly still summer's evening it could be wrought in metal, but usually it converses with a companionable rustle.

I emphasised, earlier, the importance of making plant groups in a border, so as to avoid the fidgets, but the taller, clump-forming grasses are something of an exception. Single clumps among lower neighbours can make a powerful impression. And there is a symmetry about a solo plant which may be lost when several are grown close together so that they interfere with one another at their points of contact. In a very large planting scheme such as you would expect in a public garden, grouping becomes necessary, but in our own private gardens, even when of quite a size, seldom.

And so, if your border has considerable depth, bring your grasses to or near the margin or to a corner or promontory. Don't be inhibited by the old rule, tallest at the back, shortest at the front. That, once learned, should be freely broken. The tall parts of grasses are, most usually, the inflorescences and they tend to be of diaphanous texture. You can see through them to lower plants beyond. To take some examples:

The tallest we can grow is the giant reed grass, *Arundo donax*. In a warm summer it will soar to 15 feet but it is still self supporting. Its leaves are broadish and a beautiful shade of blue. At Wisley (appropriate to mention in a Wisley Handbook), it is grown at the back of the double borders (mixed but not wholeheartedly mixed) on the way up to Battleston Hill. With a tall beech hedge immediately behind them, they make scarcely any impression. If brought halfway to the front they would stand forth as they should. In an island bed, however, this grass could be near the centre and make its presence quite sufficiently felt. I have recently planted one in the midst of a largish colony of hydrangeas and there is another, already established, near to their margin.

I have already mentioned *Miscanthus floridulus*. Of *M. sinensis* 'Silver Feather' it should additionally be said that it is, to date (but this will change), the one clone within this genus so far grown in this country that can be relied upon to flower well before the autumn. The others can and should still be grown as foliage plants but they cannot be relied upon to flower properly before the end of their growing season. Not in this country. *Miscanthus sinensis* 'Gracillimus' has very narrow leaves with a pale median stripe. It grows about 5 feet tall and dies off warm russet, so that it continues to look beautiful into the New Year.

There are two zebra grasses, both of this species and seldom distinguished in the trade which lumps them both under 'Zebrinus'. Their leaves in both cases are interrupted across a green blade by patches of yellow, faint early in the season but becoming increasingly distinct, especially in a sunny position. The habit of 'Zebrinus' is loose, with arching foliage, whereas in 'Strictus' growth is stiffer, the leaves pointing obliquely upwards. Both are good. 'Strictus' is the hardier. 'Variegatus', a 4-footer, is extremely pretty, being variegated longitudinally with pale cream marginal stripes. It makes an excellent solo specimen but I do think it contrasts marvellously with the broad foliage of a purple-leaved canna like 'Wyoming' or *Canna indica* 'Purpurea'. They are both approximately the same height and so, rather than plant them side by side, I would allow a gap in which a patch of some quite low-growing plant could link them. It could be the grey shrub *Helichrysum splendidum* (see p. 27), or perhaps a patch of white-flowered busy lizzies, e.g. *Impatiens* 'Futura White', an F_1 strain.

Stipa gigantea loves a light soil, sand or chalk. Clumps that begin to die out in patches should be replanted in late spring. Never disturb your grasses in autumn unless they belong to some other member of the household whom you wish to kill by proxy. This is another clumpy grass, its low foliage totally undistinguished, but its flowering stems run up to 6 feet and they resemble an oat but

Above: A fountain of *Miscanthus sinensis* 'Variegatus' with *Spiraea* 'Goldflame', 30 June.
Below: Important grass features, *Calamagrostis × acutiflora* 'Stricta' with pampas *Cortaderia selloana* 'Pumila' on either side, 21 Oct.

with much wider sprays and each unit therein distinct so that they make a diaphanous, rose-tinted gauze, marvellous seen against low sunlight. That is at midsummer but the display lasts as the flowers bleach with age. Get this on or near a promontory or corner.

So also *Molina caerulea altissima* 'Windspiel', which again has long, flowering stems above low groundwork. It may be outside your border's main season as it flowers in autumn, as does *M.*

Above: Liriope muscari and *Colchicum* 'The Giant', 9 Sept.
Below: Beth Chatto Water Garden, with *Eupatorium purpureum*, two miscanthus, *Gunnera chilensis*, 31 Aug.

caerulea 'Variegata'. This, however, has interesting greenish-yellow-variegated foliage but the haze of purple flowers is charming. They are only 2 feet tall. It is still an excellent corner or promontory plant and you can group it but allow 18 inches between clumps so that they do not interfere one with another.

For grass fans, I strongly recommend *Calamagrostis* × *acutiflora* 'Stricta', to make an upstanding 6 foot feature among lower flowers or foliage. I have ferns around mine but they are in full sunshine, as the grass should be. It makes a forest of dead-straight flowering stems to its full height and the inflorescence is soft mole and grey squirrel at first, bleaching as it dies to straw and remaining an asset for quite five months.

Pampas grass is not necessarily easy to accommodate in a mixed border because its saw-edged leaves spread outwards and are unkind to its neighbours. Best, given fairly dense plantings, is *Cortaderia selloana* 'Pumila', whose leaves are reasonably short. Its upright brushes are cream, with a sheen on them when young and they develop (to 5 feet or so) in late September, so this would be an unacceptable passenger in a July-August border.

Most of the grasses I have described are pretty tall, but if not of spreading habit, this need not deter the owners of small gardens. A grass for them, however, is *Hakonechloa macra* 'Aureola'. It is only a foot tall and its abundance of yellow, green-striped leaves arch outwards leaving the centre open like the crown of a Shidsu dog's head. This is a plant that takes time to establish but does not then need disturbing.

Carex stricta 'Bowles's Golden', *Glyceria maxima* 'Variegata' and *Phalaris arundinacea* 'Picta' have it in common that they will grow under water but, equally, can be used as border plants. In which position the last two are rather similar, with green and white variegation and a running rootstock. *Glyceria* is the more invasive but can be treated as a bedding plant. *Phalaris*, called gardener's garters or ribbon grass, becomes tired looking when it has run up to flower in July. I like to cut it all to the ground and let it sprout again. The carex, a sedge, makes clumps of golden-variegated leaves that are brightest in early summer but last well and harmonise with orange and yellow flowers, while providing a contrast of form.

Pennisetum are grown for their flowers which are soft and fluffy like a woolly bear caterpillar. *Pennisetum orientale*, although only 15 inches high, makes a mound of blossom rose tinted at first becoming grey, which still looks best if not closed in by tall neighbours. Charming with the pink dandelion flowers of *Crepis incana*. *Pennisetum villosum* can be and usually is treated as an annual. It is prolific in its flowers which, at Sissinghurst Castle, are specially effective at the border's front with *Sedum* 'Autumn Joy' and the grey, pinnate foliage of *Senecio leucostachys*, which is a tender shrub.

I had always wondered what to plant with *Ophiopogon planiscapus* 'Nigrescens', so as to pep up and show off its ultra dark, purple-black strap leaves, which never rise far off the ground. In the USA I saw the answer. It was interplanted with a foot-tall, prick-eared grass, *Imperata cylindrica* 'Rubra', in which the reddish blades are constantly shot through with sunlight so that they glow like rubies, but especially late and early in the day. This again would make a good planting on a border's promontory, although a small border where nothing was very high or any marginal position would serve.

Bamboos do not die back in the winter. They are shrubby grasses. Some, with a furiously running rootstock, are quite unfit for polite society. That is to say they will not mix with anything although in themselves they may, like the sasas, be quite beautiful. Others may be clump-forming as a rule and these make good mixers. But you can never be quite sure, even then. A bamboo that is generally clump-forming may, if it finds itself in rich moist soil and the weather unusually warm, suddenly behave quite differently. I would normally, in Britain, recommend the genus *Phyllostachys* as being among the most handsome and reliably behaving of bamboos. But I have recently seen how it can go berserk where the summers are warm (this was in North Carolina). Perhaps even in south Devon I might be surprised at its performance compared with east Sussex.

Anyway, assuming that *Phyllostachys* are for you and that, should they wander a little, you will have no difficulty in chopping out the errant pieces, *P. nigra* in its several varieties is strongly to be recommended. It grows to about 10 feet and presents itself stylishly. *Phyllostachys viridiglaucescens* is a good do-er to cut your teeth on and see whether these bamboos are for you. It grows to 15 feet (depending, again, on your climate) and is of pleasingly cheerful yellow-green colouring. It increases in girth faster than most. *Phyllostachys bambusoides* and *P. flexuosa* are unsuitable in a mixed border because their canes splay outwards and get in the way of neighbouring plants.

Of the tall, hardy *Arundinaria*, *A. murielae* has a better, more upstanding habit (to 8 or 10 feet) than the over-flexible *A. nitida*. Also it remains more compact, but will make a very large clump in time and may need reducing at the margins. It has the advantage (sometimes) of availability. Nurserymen in this country are making only the feeblest efforts to supply stocks of *Phyllostachys*.

Bamboos do repay a little looking after, by cutting out, each spring, dead or tired old canes. A thinned out clump looks as smart as a thick-coated dog after being stripped.

A stylish dwarf bamboo, only 2 to 2½ feet tall, of strong appearance and with little propensity to running is *Shibatea kumasasa*. It does like plenty of moisture.

A much more slender-caned but only slightly running bamboo and then only if it really likes you, is *Arundinaria viridistriata* (*A. auricoma*), whose leaves are striped in yellow and green. It looks much its brightest and freshest if cut to the ground every year, in April, and it will then grow no more that 2 feet high. For the border margin, then. I have it next to the glaucous foliage (and white flowers) of seakale, *Crambe maritima*, while behind it is a dark, solid block of *Mahonia* 'Undulata', with wavy-margined and exceptionally shiny evergreen foliage.

Another good low one is *A. variegata*, with lively green and white variegation. It could grow more than 3 feet tall, if allowed to, but I keep it to 2 foot by cutting it back every second or third year. When established, this can run quite a bit, but very charmingly. The insidious nature of the beast is to send a long, branching rhizome horizontally underground to a distance of 3 or 4 feet from the main colony, and it may go through the roots of a shrub, like a rose, which is awkward. Especially as you see no sign of what is happening until the next year, when the first above-ground shoots are made. A bit of exploratory digging round your official clump each winter is to be recommended.

There are two excellent plants, sometimes mistaken for bamboos, that are worth bringing in at this point. *Danaë racemosa* is actually related to asparagus (I am often tempted to eat its young shoots). Its branching stems are luxuriantly clothed in pointed, glossy green foliage, which is evergreen, but each stem lives only for a couple of years and so you must help the plant to rejuvenate itself. Stems that you cut out, in spring, may still be quite fresh and look well arranged with daffodils. In fact I grow the early 'February Gold' among my danaë, which are only a little taller themselves. This plant is highly shade tolerant. Sometimes it produces the odd bright orange berry and you wish it would do more.

Nandina domestica is a shrub to 3 or 4 feet with large leaves that are finely divided into elegant lanceolate leaflets, coppery when young. The white flower trusses are unimportant but a bonus. In warmer climates they are followed by spectacular crops of red berries. Better not to think about them.

Ferns

Ferns are particularly appropriate for growing among and underneath shrubs, whether deciduous or evergreen. You tolerate a shrub for so long, clothed with branches to ground level. Then, as its bulk increases, you think 'this is getting too much' and you remove its lowest branches so that it becomes a tree in miniature, albeit a many-stemmed tree. Now you can plant again, right into its centre.

An *Olearia macrodonta* will serve as an example. It is one of the New Zealand daisy bushes with evergrey-green holly-like leaves, with mock prickles and masses of clustered white flowers in June. Mine grew, from a baby out of a 5 inch pot, far bigger than I ever anticipated and would, if permitted, have engulfed a path on one side and a strip of lawn on the other. Between is the border in which it grew. So I made a 'tree' of it, as I have described, some 9 feet high and far more across. It had beautiful peeling trunks. Underneath I grew the spring-flowering perennial, *Omphalodes cappadocica*, that resembles a large forget-me-not; an anemone, *Anemone hortensis*, with purple flowers in spring; the late flowering cranesbill, *Geranium wallichianum* 'Buxton's Blue'; *Campanula persicifolia*, which seeded itself where it wanted to be and poked out of the olearia's sides; finally, on either side of the bush, a rather precious evergreen fern, *Polystichum setiferum* 'Pulcherrimum Bevis', which is a mutant of the soft shield fern. All these are shade lovers, so I was thrown, somewhat, when the olearia (over a period of two years) died. Shrubby members of the Compositae are rather apt to do this, I find.

So, from being shade lovers my underplantings had to become sun baskers and they took this change of role absolutely in their stride.

In another instance I had *Blechnum chilense*, which is a carpeting, colonising fern, underneath a tree peony, *Paeonia delavayi*. That died of peony botrytis but the fern looks even better in the sun. Although its fronds are shorter, they grow more densely and their colouring from youth to maturity (new fronds appearing all through the summer) is much more varied in sun, starting coppery and maturing deep green.

I am not trying to suggest that all ferns are as happy in the sun as the shade. Some do scorch badly in a blazing position; the shuttlecock fern, *Matteuccia struthiopteris*, for instance. My point is that it is generally very useful to be able to grow ferns in shade but it may, at times, also be useful to grow them in sun and it should not be assumed that this is stupid.

As with the grasses, you can, culturally, divide ferns into clump formers and colonisers. Polystichums are among the best of the clump formers. A great many variations on the theme have turned up over the years. Within *P. setiferum* these have been subdivided into the Acutilobum and the Divisilobum groups. The first have narrow, sharply pointed pinnules (the smallest subdivision of a frond), leaving spaces between, as in a grill or lattice screen. They are quite strong growers and clumps should never be planted so closely that the fronds of one grow into the fronds of another. This simply looks confused. Leave at least 3 feet between them and interplant with early bulbs. The old fronds should anyhow be cut away (generally in March but it can, for the sake of your bulb display, be done in the New Year) before the new ones unfurl, otherwise it is difficult to do the job without damaging the new in removing the old. If you don't do it at all, the ruff of old fronds will, as spring progresses, increasingly take from the beauty of the new.

That goes for any evergreen fern, such as *Blechnum*, *Polypodium*, *Asplenium scolopendrium* (the hartstongue) and other polystichums.

The Divisilobum group of *Polystichum setiferum* includes the Plumosum (feathery) types and all are soft, even mossy-textured.

Hartstongue ferns have a special value in their perfectly plain strap leaves, which can be contrasted with the more typically divided frond. In general, ferns of different kinds look better when not grown together, which leads to a certain monotony that confuses the eye, but in conjunction with quite different plants. Hosta leaves would generally make a striking contrast but ferns have such a presence of their own that you would do better to grow quite dwarf hostas among or close to them, rather than the dominant kinds which would compete at the ferns' own level.

Small things like celandines (*Ranunculus ficaria*), hepaticas, *Hacquetia epipactis* (with tiny yellow flowers surrounded by a green ruff), primroses and anemones make ideal companions. Later in the season, blocks of a colonising fern like *Polypodium vulgare* 'Cornubiense' look good alternating with fairly low growing hardy fuchsias, as it might be 'Tom Thumb' or 'Lady Thumb', 'Alice Hofman' or 'Poppet'. Hardy cyclamen, especially *Cyclamen hederifolium*, go well with dwarf ferns like *Blechnum penna-marina*.

You will often find that a wild fern, usually *Dryopteris filix-mas*, the male fern, has sown itself at the base of a shrub in your border. Take the hint. If it puts itself there it is a place where a more interesting fern will flourish. You can make the exchange.

Bulbs

Auxiliaries rather than protagonists is my attitude to bulbs in a mixed border, although there are exceptions. They lengthen the season at both ends without being allowed to detract from the main display, which I shall continue to assume to be in the height of summer.

You could regard them as an extension of your bedding out activities, in which case the spring flowerers would need to be removed at the end of May and replaced with annuals and summer bedding. I prefer to regard bulbs as permanencies in the mixed border. They should be sited where they seldom need to be disturbed, among perennials or underneath the skirts of shrubs. Since bulbs are out of sight for much of the year, it is wise to mark their positions, as you plant them, with short pieces of cane. Then, when next you're working in that area, the canes will remind you that there is something underneath. You could use a label, but nowadays I prefer to rely upon a note at the time of planting in my garden book.

The earliest bulbs go well beneath or among deciduous shrubs, completing their growth before the shrubs are casting much shade. Snowdrops (*Galanthus*) build into fat clumps and seed themselves freely, even under a rooty old lilac. A crocus like *Crocus tommasinianus* will seed itself so generously that you will find yourself digging up its corms in the dead season. Not to worry, just push the exposed corms back into the ground with the tip of your finger. Among a strong but spreading grower like *Geranium endressii* or *G. sanguineum*, *C. tommasinianus* can seed and cohabit without doing any harm. Its leaves are narrow enough not to look too bad for too long as they die off.

Scillas flower in March and are happy spreaders. I have planted a rich blue *Scilla bifolia* with the hardy perennial *Valeriana phu* 'Aurea', whose leaves are bright lime green, almost yellow, early in the season. *Scilla sibirica* is the brightest and best known species ('Spring Beauty' is indistinguishable from it) and colonises well among fuchsias, ceratostigmas, *Potentilla fruticosa*, perovskias and suchlike late developing shrubs that can be cut back in late winter or spring. I saw an interesting mixed planting that covered a long season at Brookside Gardens in Maryland. Overhead were purple-leaved *Prunus cerasifera* cut hard back annually for maximum foliage impact on a large shrub rather than a tree.

Underneath was continuous cover at the foot-tall level of *Ceratostigma plumbaginoides*. This has deep blue, plumbago-type flowers in late summer and autumn and the leaves colour up well. It is a ground cover plant that gradually increases its range by suckering. With and underneath this (and the ceratostigma can all be cut away in winter) is a mass planting of tiny bulbs like scillas and chionodoxas, crocus and erythroniums – anything of low stature except for the grape hyacinth, *Muscari armenaicum*, whose lank foliage has a disagreeable habit of appearing in the autumn.

If you include *Narcissus*, restrict yourself to those kinds, mostly dwarfs, whose leaves are slender and will not, in May, make your border look as though it had finished for the year, when it has not even begun. Such is the 10-inch-tall 'Hawera', a *N. triandrus* hybrid, neat, multiflowered, pale yellow. A very late flowerer like the yellow, jonquil-style 'Tittle Tattle', mixes well in a group of day lilies, because by the time its own foliage is looking ratty, the hemerocallis will have grown up enough to conceal the defect.

The May-flowering tulips are especially suitable, for the same reason, that their foliage is already engulfed among their perennial neighbours by the time it is yellowing. It helps matters to remove the flowered stems. You can plant them among Japanese anemones, *Rudbeckia* 'Goldsturm' (a late starting black-eyed Susan, flowering from August on), lupins. Also at the front of threadbare shrubs like the summer tamarisk (see p. 24), roses, some hydrangeas, indigoferas. Late tulips that I have found particularly obliging (and they persist for 20 years or more on a stiffish soil) include the lily-flowered 'White Triumphator' and 'Redshine'; parrots 'Orange Favourite' and 'Texas Gold'; single late 'Mrs John T. Scheepers' (egg-shaped, yellow), 'Dillenburg' (orange) and 'Halcro' (soft red with a touch of pink).

Some of the summer flowering bulbs have lank, decaying foliage at, or soon after, flowering and while it may not hurt to cut it down as soon as flowering is over, it also helps to place them well into your border so that their leaves are hidden by the plants or shrubs in front. Thus, the mauve globes of *Allium giganteum* will rise importantly behind and above a solid evergreen screen of, it might be, *Cistus × corbariensis*, which itself opens pink buds into white flowers in early summer but is still a handsome bush in the depths of winter. The allium's dying foliage is all at ground level.

The early summer flowering *Gladiolus byzantinus*, with magenta spikes, can nestle up against something like border phloxes, whose growth will soon expand and fill in where you have removed the gladiolus evidence. Try and use the kinds with rather light spikes that do not flop around unless staked individually.

Montbretias, now called *Crocosmia*, can make permanent

groups like any perennial and flower at the height of summer.

Alstroemeria ligtu hybrids are a special case. They carry a wonderful display of azalea-like blossom in late June and early July. After that they quickly become an eyesore but because their tubers go deep into the soil, you can plant above them with a late summer replacement, as it might be *Lobelia* 'Queen Victoria', *Salvia patens* or African marigolds held in reserve (they will move from the open ground). All you have to do by way of preparation is to give a sharp tug to all the old alstroemeria stems. They break cleanly, 6 inches or so below the soil surface, leaving the area clear.

Galtonia candicans, the Cape hyacinth, is stiff, with a naked stem to 4 feet high with its waxy white bells in July-August. When I have planted it well into a border it seems to like to seed itself into the marginal parts and I believe in taking a hint. Try planting it sporadically, rather than in a heavy clump, so that it mixes in with plants mentioned earlier that also go well together: *Eryngium giganteum*, *Lychnis coronaria*, *Fuchsia magellanica* 'Versicolor'. The odd plant of sea lavender, *Limonium latifolium*, with a haze of mauve blossom in August above heavy green leaves, would work in here well, also.

The only lilies that I find persist through the years in my heavy slug-infested soil are the purple and white martagons (*Lilium martagon* and *L. m.* 'Album'), and the tall apricot-coloured *L. henryi*. *Lilium regale*, with its scented white trumpets in July, is excellent on lighter soils. Don't mass any of these, or you'll notice they're doing nothing for you too much of the time. Interplant low shrubs and perennials with them. You can insert an informal line of them behind hostas, whose foliage will spread into their positions at a lowish level.

Of the autumn flowering bulbs, I would not be without some clumps of colchicums. They flower in August-September and their big glossy leaves are lush and handsome in spring. As they yellow, in late May or early June, you must cut them away, before you start grumbling at their unsightliness, and you can either interplant them for the next two or three months with a quick-developing annual like *Dimorphotheca* or *Brachycome* (the Swan river daisy), or allow neighbouring grey-leaved foliage plants of a rambling habit to fill in of their own accord. *Artemisia canescens* (hardy) or *Helichrysum petiolatum* (tender) would meet the occasion.

Nerine × *bowdenii* needs no special baking to make it flower and its pink umbels on 18 inch stems are cheering in September-October. I interplant them with the purple michaelmas daisy, *Aster amellus* 'Violet Queen', which grows to the same height or slightly under and also flowers in autumn. But these will be summer passengers. You may have a brighter idea.

Tender perennials

This class of plant has to be overwintered under cover or, if left out, its owner must appreciate that a calculated risk is being taken. Safe overwintering will either be by the storage, generally in darkness, of a fleshy, nutrient-rich root or rhizome; or by taking cuttings in the autumn and keeping them under frost-free glass. Sometimes an entire shrubby plant is lifted and returned to the safety of a greenhouse, but this is expensive in terms of space as against the cuttings method, which allows old plants to be discarded. Besides which you rejuvenate your stock by starting again from cuttings rather than saving a woody old lag which may well have lost its zest for growing strongly.

Many of these tender perennials have a prolonged season of flowering or of foliage glamour. They may introduce colours, like red, which are in short supply among the hardies. And they have a lushness which contributes an air of summer opulence to your border.

Dahlias are the most obvious example. Rather than dot them about in any gap that seems to be available at planting time in late spring, but which often does not exist in reality once the border has grown, make special provision for them so that there is space to plant them in groups of one variety, just as you would phloxes or delphiniums.

Dahlias need stout stakes, one to each plant, and stakes are not beautiful objects. Insist that they are of a neutral colour, not that virulent, unnatural shade of green imparted by wood preserving 'Cuprinol' as sometimes sold. Clear 'Cuprinol' is also available and is colourless. Again, it is preferable to have your dahlias growing strongly in their positions before you stake them. That cuts down on the time it will take them to conceal their stakes altogether.

Their tubers in winter need to be stored in a cold but frost free place, as you would potatoes. If their tubers are spindly, not plump, at lifting, they are all to liable to shrivel and it is safer to box them up in old potting soil and give them a watering through the dormant season, say once a week.

This is always the treatment for *Salvia patens*, which makes a cluster of thin tubers. When you see them beginning to sprout in spring, either plant them out or, if the place is occupied, place their box in a cold frame in a light spot. This salvia normally has deep blue flowers on a 2 foot plant, and there is also a Cambridge blue strain. It can alternatively be raised from seed and treated as an annual.

Cannas make fleshy rhizomes in the autumn. Lift their clumps entire and pack them with some extra soil into a deep wooden box. Don't let them dry right out. The clumps, if huge or if you want more stock, can be broken up at planting out in June, by which time they will be growing strongly and have plenty of roots. Cannas are splendid foliage plants, green, purple or variegated, and those with large silken flowers in shades of red, pink or yellow, will do you proud in a hot season. They need no staking.

You can also make special provision, in your border, for those tender perennials which are propagated from cuttings (say 10 to a 3½-inch pot) and overwintered like that, potting them off individually in the spring and hardening them up in a cold frame. As an example, I recently had a patch at the front of my border of a Verbena × hybrida clone 'Pink Bouquet', with a rosy red bedding Penstemon, 'Drinkstone Red', behind it. They were taking the place of Monarda 'Cambridge Scarlet', which I had lost in the winter. Verbenas can be raised from seed, but the named clones are sometimes superior to a mixed batch of seedlings, and these must be raised from cuttings. Same story with the penstemons. But they will sometimes survive the winter, in which case the technique is to cut them very hard back in April, when you see new growth appearing at the base. They will then flower to beat the band in early summer, but not a lot thereafter. It might be worth replacing them with late-sown annuals in July.

Various daisies are included among tender perennials. Chrysanthemum frutescens, the Paris daisy, has colourful clones such as 'Jamaica Primrose' and the pink, anemone-centred 'Vancouver'. Chrysanthemum foeniculaceum is a white daisy but with excellent lacy foliage of glaucous hue. Euryops chrysanthemoides is covered with daisies all summer of a clear, sharp yellow. Osteospermum 'Buttermilk' is one of several South African daisies, somewhat bushy in habit, this one pale yellow. That known as 'Ecklonis Prostrata' is mat-forming and will creep out over paving from a marginal planting. White, blue-eyed daisies with a mauve reverse.

The rambling habit of Helichrysum petiolatum, with felted heart-shaped leaves, makes an ideal gap filler of this foliage plant. Another that gives quick returns is the grey, double-comb-leaved Senecio leucostachys.

Biennials

The most important biennials for mixed border work are foxgloves, mulleins, stocks, sweet williams, honesty, forget-me-nots and evening primroses. I exclude canterbury bells (*Campanula medium*) because they go over so quickly and the dead blooms hang on. First to flower are *Myosotis*, the forget-me-nots and they have a long season, up to the very end of May, at which stage you should pull out all those that are still visible and forget (sorry, yes, forget) about those which have become engulfed in rapidly growing perennials. Forget-me-nots are, indeed, most useful for filling in between plants of phloxes, for instance, which will not themselves be inhibited by their proximity. But watch it when myosotis seed themselves (as, in the mixed border context, we depend upon them to do after the first introduction) among small plants which they can easily engulf and kill. When overhauling your border in autumn or spring, therefore, weed out any plants that you can see will later be a nuisance. Leave those that will extend your border's season. When they're flowering, swivel a sharp eye on to them again, making sure there's no mischief afoot.

Lunaria annua, which we call honesty, the American money plant, likewise. They self-sow like crazy but, being shade tolerant, give excellent value beneath and among shrubs, as it might be lilac or the suckering *Clerodendron bungei*, which carries domes of rich carmine, scented flowers above luxuriant heart-shaped foliage in late summer and autumn. The white honesty and the two variegated kinds, one with white flowers, the other with mauve, but both with a pale cream variegation, show up especially well in shade. But you must keep them separate, otherwise they will not come true from seed. All flower in May.

Foxgloves, *Digitalis purpurea*, are likewise excellent value in shade, beneath tall shrubs or trees, but they are June flowering. You can allow them to maintain themselves by self-sowing but this becomes unsatisfactory over a period of years because they tend to revert to the wild, pinkish purple colouring, which does not show up too well from a distance in the garden and clashes abominably with any orange flowers. The apricot and white digitalis strains would be my first choice, although the giant spotted kinds are great fun. I do not consider that the Excelsior hybrids, which display their flowers horizontally, have any particular advantages. Foxgloves passing out of bloom are ugly and the plants should be pulled out as this stage approaches. You need annuals in reserve to take their place.

I believe in raising foxgloves, sweet williams and mulleins properly, so as to obtain the finest plants. Sow in a pot in April under cold glass; prick off the seedlings, 28 or 40 to a tray. Then line them out, 15 inches apart in a spare plot for the summer. Move them into their flowering positions in the autumn.

Sweet williams, *Dianthus barbatus*, are all too often scattered about through a border and then left to run to seed after flowering, which is most unsightly, since their season ends in the second half of July and they need a follow-on. This is much more convenient to provide if the sweet williams are given a patch in your border to themselves. You can interplant them with tulips. Lift the whole lot in late July, harvesting the bulbs and discarding the sweet willies and replant with an annual or bedding dahlias, sown in May. If you sow sweet williams too late, they only flower at half cock in the following year. April is best, and the plants, when growing them on, can be sprayed with a copper fungicide to prevent an attack of rust on their foliage.

The most dramatic of the biennial mulleins is *Verbascum olympicum*, which soars to 8 feet (give it a stake in case of high winds) and has a great branching candelabrum of yellow blossom. Be sure to spray (or handpick twice daily for a week) the handsome but destructive caterpillars of the mullein shark moth while they are still small, in early June. *Verbascum bombyciferum*, also called 'Silver Lining', or 'Silver Spire', has beautiful, felted, pale grey foliage which is at its most striking in the rosette stage in the first year and as the spike is running up in the late spring of the second. In flower it is less well balanced than *V. olympicum* (and so is *V. phlomoides*, which is sometimes sold as *V. olympicum*).

A number of the evening primroses are biennials and can be allowed to self-sow. The least weedy looking in habit, indeed it can be statuesque, is *Oenothera erythrosepala*, sometimes known as *O. lamarckiana*. It grows to 6 foot and opens its great bowl-shaped yellow chalices at dusk. They last into the next forenoon.

Stocks (*Matthiola*) of the Brompton strain can be bedded into your border from a late spring sowing, in the autumn and will be at their best the following late May and June (to be followed, of course, by annuals). Their scent is delicious and the single-flowered kinds mix pleasantly with doubles. They are happiest on light soils. On heavy ground they tend to go down to botrytis in the spring of the second year and it is worth treating them with Benlate in solution, from a watering can, in the New Year and again in March.

Lupins can be treated as biennials in the same way as foxgloves, sweet williams and stocks, being followed by annuals.

Annuals

Few annuals have much structure to them (*Nicotiana sylvestris*, *Polygonum orientale* and *Cleome spinosa* are obvious exceptions) and a bed or border devoted to them alone suffers from this defect. Also it has a tendency to pack too much colour, indigestibly, into a small space. In a mixed border their colour may have great advantages, while other kinds of plants will provide the elements of shape, texture and solidity.

Tall annuals are useful for replacing the biennials I have just been describing when they have done their turn. Also for filling a big gap left by a shrub that has died unexpectedly. My enormous specimen of *Solanum crispum* 'Glasnevin', with a host of mauve potato flowers in summer, died one year after flowering, without leaving the customary suicide note. I have since filled in with annuals and biennials and so enjoy the gap that I have no immediate intention of a permanent planting. That is one of the lovely things about annuals and biennials. You can change your mind so quickly about which to use and about changes to make next year. Happy armchair hours with catalogues arise from this plotting in the depths of winter when your mind needs lifting out of the present. Some people do it with travel brochures. Gardeners can bring exotica to their own doorsteps.

Nicotiana sylvestris, with large, rich green paddle leaves and heads of long-tubed white flowers, deliciously night scented, is an excellent follow-on to foxglove or honesty in a rather shady but moist and well fed situation.

To replace lupins and verbascums in an open site, I choose from a number of favourites. *Tithonia rotundifolia* 'Torch' is like a giant zinnia with glowing orange flowers. The dwarfer 'Goldfinger' has not nearly its style or presence. *Cosmos bipinnatus*, with its feathery foliage on a 4 to 5 foot plant (give each a cane and a tie and space them at 2 feet), comes in various pink and carmine shades, usually mixed, but is most attractive, I think, in the pure white 'Purity', which also has paler green leaves.

Lavatera trimestris 'Loveliness' and 'Tanagra' are excellent pink mallows but a trifle brash in colouring. The soft rosy red *Malope trifida* 'Grandiflora' is a close relation. The green calyx shines like stained glass window slits in the base of each funnel flower. Stake as for cosmos, as also the sweet scabious *Scabiosa atropurpurea*.

This is best sown in early autumn and overwintered in individual pots under cold glass, planting out in spring, thus bringing forward the onset of its otherwise tardy flowering to July. The spider flower, *Cleome spinosa*, has palmate leaves like a horsechesnut and pink, white or bright mauve flowers on an indefinitely lengthening stem that continues over a long period. Never starve this as a seedling, or it won't recover.

Polygonum orientale has dropped out of the lists so I must write about it to get it back. It makes an elegant 4 foot plants (but beware slugs) of a branching habit covered with drooping spikelets of deep carmine flowers.

The castor oil, *Ricinus communis*, is grown for its bold, palmate leaves which are most striking in the purple-leaved 'Gibsonii'. In a warm summer this may grow to 5 or 6 feet. Much depends on the season (as also for tithonias).

Dahlias treated as annuals also make excellent follow-ons. If the plants are not needed until late June or up to the end of July, you must delay your sowings till some time in May and keep the young plants happy by potting them individually, even into 5-inch pots if the wait is a long one. Then, when you do plant them out, they will be ready to go into immediate action.

African marigolds (*Tagetes erecta*), the large growing, widely branching kinds like 'Climax' and 'Toreador', are of special value in a mixed border because they are imposing plants (unlike the Inca series with large blooms on a small plant, which looks totally unbalanced). From a late April or May sowing under cold glass they can be lined out in a spare plot until needed and, given a good soaking before and after, moved into their final positions as large plants already coming into flower.

There are many delightful, natural looking annuals to use near a border's margin. Direct sowings are seldom as satisfactory as raising plants under controlled conditions initially (sun heat is quite sufficient and an April sowing early enough), pricking out the seedlings into, for preference, deep boxes, not more than 40, often only 28 to a box. You can use soilless or John Innes composts, both of which will be weed-free. In the latter case, sow and prick out into J.I. potting compost No. 1 (the seed compost is necessary only for early sowings when days are short and sunlight weak).

Of the shorter annuals with a long flowering season I would recommend the bushy, 1 foot, *Cuphea miniata* 'Firefly', which is pinky-red and has a prettily shaped flower. *Anagallis linifolia* in its blue form is as intensely coloured as a gentian and often mistaken for one. It is almost prostrate and grows about 6 inches high. *Calceolaria mexicana* is an elegant species, to 2 feet smothered in flattened pouches of a nice acid, palish yellow. Once grown it will self-sow year after year. *Brachycome iberidifolia* is the Swan river daisy, usually seen in mixtures: blue, purple, mauve and white; swarms of blossom on 9 inch plants with fine-spun leaves.

Other self-seeders include *Nemophila maculata*, a hardy annual whose seedlings appear in the autumn. Bowl-shaped, palest mauve flowers in May, each petal having a deep purple spot at its tip. Love-in-a-mist, *Nigella damascena*, deserves to be grown in a pure blue strain, as we have few enough blues, but the purplish *N. hispanica* is a striking species. *Alonsoa warscewiczii* looks less weedy in its 18 inch-tall compact strain. It has pale scarlet flowers over a long season. The annual grass, *Briza maxima*, with flowers like dangling lockets, should not be omitted though its self-sown seedlings will need thinning out each autumn.

Like the forget-me-nots, these self-sowers can weave in among other plants, weeding out only those that will be a nuisance to a more permanent neighbour; or they can grow over the bare patch left in summer by bulbs like colchicums and sternbergias that are resting.

ENVOI

Mixed borders, once you get the hang of the idea, become a way of life and there are many directions in which you can steer your own particular craft. Your temperament will decide the direction taken and you will be revealing a piece of yourself through your art, which gardening is.

This book makes suggestions and offers help, from my experience, of ways and means. Once the reader has got his own ideas, he will be able to dispense with me altogether, but I hope now and again to be allowed to see and enjoy the results.

Approximate conversion table

inches	centimetres	feet	metres
$\frac{3}{4}$	2	1	0.3
1	3	$1\frac{1}{2}$	0.5
$1\frac{1}{2}$	4	2	0.6
2	5	$2\frac{1}{2}$	0.8
$2\frac{1}{4}$	6	3	0.9
$2\frac{3}{4}$	7		
3	8		
$3\frac{1}{2}$	9		
4	10		
12	30		

Index of plant names